"READ!"

The Reality Behind Muhammad's First Revelation

AHMED HULUSI

As with all my works, this book is not copyrighted.
As long as it remains faithful to the original,
it may be freely printed, reproduced, published and translated.
For the knowledge of ALLAH, there is no recompense.

"READ!"

The Reality Behind Muhammad's First Revelation

AHMED HULUSI

www.ahmedhulusi.org/en/

Translated by ALIYA ATALAY

ABOUT THE COVER

The black background of the front cover represents darkness and ignorance, while the white color of the letters represents light and knowledge.

The image is a Kufi calligraphy of the Word of Unity: *"La ilaha illallah; Muhammad Rasulullah"* which means,

"There is no concept such as 'god', there is only that which is denoted by the name Allah, and **Muhammad (SAW)** is the *Rasul* of this understanding."

The placement of the calligraphy, being on top and above everything else on the page, is a symbolic representation of the predominant importance this understanding holds in the author's life.

The green light, reflecting from the window of the Word of Unity, opens up from the darkness into luminosity to illustrate the light of Allah's *Rasul*. This light is embodied in the book's title through the author's pen and concretized as the color white, to depict the enlightenment the author aims to attain in this field. As the knowledge of Allah's *Rasul* disseminates, those who are able to evaluate this knowledge attain enlightenment, which is represented by the white background of the back cover.

CONTENTS

INTRODUCTION

Dear thinking minds…

In this book I hope to present you with a totally unique perspective. As the title suggests, I'm going to explore 'what Muhammad (saw) read' – not literally, but *actually*.

As known, Muhammad retreated to a cave at the top of Mount Hira after a series of events he experienced over a period of two years. It was at this time the angel Gabriel (as) appeared to him and told him:

READ!

But he wasn't given a written text to read!

Muhammad (saw) told the angel Gabriel, "I'm not of those who can read; I can't read…"

But, again he was told to "READ".

Since there was no paper or parchment or any other form of written text he could read, clearly this wasn't about the kind of reading that we know of!

From this we can deduce that the concept of being 'illiterate' does not mean the inability to read, as commonly known.

So, what does it mean to be illiterate or unlettered?

Who are the unlettered?

How can one avoid being illiterate?

Was Muhammad (saw), who couldn't read because he was unlettered, still regarded as unlettered after he obeyed the command 'READ'?

Dear thinking minds…

In this book I shall try to explain the answers to these questions, as much as my observations allow, and without overly disturbing our friends who'd rather accept what has been narrated to them without too much thought…

Surely, everything I write is within the scope of the knowledge and observation my Rabb has bestowed me and surely beyond everyone that knows there are those who know more.

If I could aid my friends to take one step further in terms of knowledge, I will be thankful to my Rabb for enabling me with this opportunity.

I hope and pray that Allah allows us to constantly rise higher on the infinite steps of knowledge and to apply this knowledge in our day-to-day lives.

So, join me in exploring the secrets of the universe and discovering what Muhammad (saw) read…

Ahmed Hulusi

1

THE TRUTH OF THE UNIVERSE

My dear friends,

Before I delve into the main topic of our book, I want to share some evaluations in light of modern science…

There's a question that mankind has been asking for centuries that hasn't been answered yet:

What is the universe, who am I, what is my relation to the universe?

Even though innumerous philosophers, scientists and Sufis have elucidated this topic in their own capacity, they've not been able to present a holistic answer to the world of thought that has satisfied everyone.

Here are some popular Sufi evaluations on the nature of the universe:

The essence of all the worlds is an illusion!

All of existence is a single makeup.

There is only the One in existence and that is Allah.

Seeing more than one is an optical defect, only the One exists.

To prevent misunderstanding, I choose to suffice with stating these are popular Sufi thoughts without referencing the names of those to whom they belong. Those who wish to may search the relevant works to find out.

Let's now try to evaluate these statements in light of modern science.

We know that man perceives the universe with his five senses. Therefore, a universe perceived by the five senses of a human is different to a universe perceived by an animal or another being, who also perceives according to its capacity of perception.

Let me try to explain this with a simple example:

The human eye receives waves between 4,000-7,000 angstroms and sends these to the brain, which are then converted to images by the brain. We think these waves, which are converted according to the brain's program, are existent, while those outside this range are nonexistent. This is where we fail to see the truth.

Even though our eyes are only able to perceive a tiny little snippet of an infinite scale of wavelengths, we confine the entire existence to that tiny section we perceive and think inside this limited box! Whereas in reality, the universe consists of an infinite ocean of waves, or quants, where what we perceive isn't even a drop in the ocean!

The other point that needs to be considered well is, if the waves between 4,000-7,000 angstroms received by our eyes are meaningful, then the entire universe with all its infinite wavelengths and dimensions comprises a meaningful integrality. Unfortunately, however, the limitation of our tools of perception deprives us of duly evaluating the integrality of the universe.

This means the conditioning to which our brain is subject causes certain blockages and limitations. The five senses, and our conditioning that we must evaluate everything based on the five senses, prevent us from perceiving the One in the guise of many!

Even though we know scientifically that, if we had a sensory device that could perceive at the atomic level, we would all be ONE.

If, for example, you can remove the roof and ceiling from the room you're in and observe it under a microscope with a billion times zoom capacity, the only thing you'll see will be a field of atoms. Thus, all the objects that are currently in the room will disappear and only a homogeneous mass comprising various atoms, such as iron, copper, zinc, hydrogen, nitrogen and oxygen, will remain.

The brain that deduces numerous objects when looking through the eyes now sees a homogeneous atomic field when looking through an electron microscope, a field in which the 'many' objects are now reduced to a hundred or so different atoms!

But, what if we were able to zoom a trillion or even quadrillion times into the room?

We would come to realize that everything we think exists in the universe is fictional existence based completely on the capacity of the means of perception.

Indeed, everything that we think exists is 'according to' the brain's limited perception, and so all the images we perceive are images of this limited range of data.

Where does this take us?

Matter – cell – molecule – atom – neutron – quark – quant – descending dimensionally to the essence brings us to such a point of oneness that nothing other than the ONE can be conceived.

In short, what we refer to as the universe is essentially such Oneness that, whatever we may call it, there's no room for another beside it.

As much as we can perceive, one of the qualities of this Oneness, which we call the universe, is pure consciousness and the other is universal energy, and it continues its existence with its own system at every instance free from the concept of time.

What we need to do, if we can, is understand our place in it.

2

THINKING IN LIGHT OF SCIENTIFIC DATA

It is now definite that the universe is an ocean of infinite waves and man is only able to perceive a very tiny section of this, due to his five senses. Thus, it's not possible to talk about 'the' universe in the absolute sense, only 'one's individual' universe in the relative sense.

So, in sight of this hard to digest reality, what does man need to do?

Determine the reality of himself and his dimension, as best as he can, in light of scientific data, while coping with the limitations brought about by the five senses... But this is where the problem begins...

No matter how much technology advances, the brain is bound to evaluate with the five senses, which means, beyond what is perceived, there are countless dimensions and in those dimensions there are innumerous values, and with those values, infinite species and forms of life!

So, when we look from a scientific perspective, we can see that, outside the scope of what we perceive to be matter, are countless other forms of life, which according to their dimension of life, are also forms of 'matter'.

Could it be that the entire existence is ethereal and only our dimension of life is material? Does the universe consist of dimensions that are made of matter and those that are not matter? Do living beings exist only in the material dimensions?

Science shows us that every level of existence, from the cosmological systems at the macrocosmic plane to the microcosmic muons and quants, is a compositional structure that leads to the creation of one another. Each of these levels of existence is material in its own scope; thus, in actuality, 'matter' and 'non-matter' aren't two different concepts, but completely relative and subject to change according to the observer.

For those whose perception is a few degrees higher than ours, our world may be 'beyond-matter,' while for those whose perception is a few degrees lower than ours, our world may not even exist.

When we can see that a cell or bacteria in our body isn't even aware of us, when we have such an example in front of us, how can we possibly think other living-conscious beings do not exist?

As far as we can perceive, whether it be in terms of wave composition or quant composition, realistic thinking brings us to the conclusion there are infinite numbers of living conscious beings in the universe... But, because we haven't been able to rid ourselves from the conditionings of matter and materialism spawned from the prematurity of the 19th century, we haven't been able to adopt the system of modern thought. This prevents us from making a leap into the realities and true values of the universe, confining us to resolve and evaluate everything on the restricted platform of matter.

We must know and understand without any doubt that every compositional being ranging from quants to what we have come to call matter, the realm of the five senses, to the levels of higher matter, has an individual consciousness and values. If we accept this truth and continue to research into this field, we may obtain the opportunity to communicate with these conscious units of existence. Denial, the expression of narrow-mindedness, will result in nothing more than blinded consciousness.

One who thinks expansively and comprehensively is one who thinks scientifically, rather than opting for denial.

The reality of life after death is based on the ethereal makeup of consciousness, which takes form at every level of existence according to its compositional structure, for consciousness is derived not from matter but from the universal origin that comprises matter.

Universal consciousness, which takes form as the body and the brain in this dimension of life, will simply take another form, either lower or higher, after death, and thus continue its existence indefinitely…

So, in light of all of this, how much can our horizon of thought transcend the plane of matter and delve into the dimensional depths beyond what we perceive to be material…?

3

OUR UNIVERSAL ESSENCE

Since man is incapable of knowing the universe with his five senses as he is a part of the very universe he perceives, and since everything in the universe is comprised of various frequencies of waves manifesting various meanings, what exactly is man?

According to those who can go beyond only that which they see with their eyes and turn to their essence, who can unblock the five sense-based data limitation of their brain and think more comprehensively towards the universal essence in light of both science and intuition... Every unit of existence in the universe contains within itself all of the values of the universal essence, based on its makeup, perception tools and level of existence. As long as these units that carry the universal essence continue to exist at the level formed by their perception that level of existence will appear to be 'matter,' while all other levels will be inexistent due to the inadequacy of their perception capacity.

Because everything in the universe is derived from the same source, whether we call it the Creative Power or Pure Consciousness, this universal power and knowledge holographically exist in every iota of every unit of existence in the universe.

If we can put aside the perception of the innumerous forms that are comprised of the same essence yet of different compositions, and look from a single point of perception, one that encompasses all other points of perception, we can view the world of forms from the point of the essence and see that nothing other than the One exists – One that is ever-living, infinite, limitless and powerful, whatever we may choose to call this Oneness.

Since the scientific evaluations of today weren't known in the previous centuries, those who were able to turn to their essence and perceive beyond the five senses in the past were able to reach these truths; however, they expressed them in their own language, using symbols and metaphors.

When they claimed, 'The universe is comprised of a single Spirit', 'everything exists and subsists with this single Spirit' and 'man needs not to search for this Spirit outside as it exists within himself' they were unfortunately not understood by those whose reality is based on their eyesight.

Since the universe is essentially one infinite consciousness and every unit exists with its own inherent knowledge and power, man can only arrive at the truth of the universe through his own self; his own essence and consciousness.

Whether we arrive at the whole or come from the whole, the priority is always the whole. If you don't know the whole, you can't arrive at what you don't know. If you don't know the whole, you can't come from the whole. So, the first thing that needs to be done, in any case, is to know the whole.

If our experience of matter is only a level of existence that depends on our five-sense perception, then every time our tool of perception changes what we call matter is also going to change. And since it's our consciousness that determines this, it is evident that consciousness is not matter.

Consciousness isn't matter; it is a wavelength of an unknown frequency comprised of the universal essence, which we are unable to fathom and evaluate at this point.

Based on this truth, we're not just one body out of trillions made of flesh and bones living on one of the planets among trillions of others in one of the galaxies among billions of others – according to our eyesight – rather, we are a unique frequency of universal essence and consciousness!

Thus, everything we've come to define as matter through the filter of our five senses is nothing other than a radial structure composed of various frequencies. In the days of old, they referred to this universal consciousness, which is holographically present in every iota of existence, as the 'spirit'.

In light of all of this, death does not in any way mean becoming inexistent; it is the leap of one's consciousness from the realm of matter to the holographic radial realm or transition to the realm of the spirit. A radial universe in which the holographic radial body will live indefinitely according to the capacity it has reached.

4

WHEN AN ILLITERATE READS

The first verse and command of the Quran is 'READ'!

But how did this command reach Muhammad (saw) and what did he feel at that moment? How did the angel Gabriel (as) come to him, ask him to 'READ' and 'squeeze' him; what was this experience like for Muhammad (saw)?

Let's see how this incident has been recorded in authentic hadith. Sahih Bukhari and Sahih Muslim narrate this hadith in the following way:

The Rasul of Allah (saw) had begun to see some powerful dreams that would actually play out; there wasn't a single dream that didn't manifest exactly the way he'd seen. In time, he grew fond of retreating. He would retreat to the top of Mount Hira and spend many nights there in servitude. For this, he would take some food with him and, when he ran out, his wife Khadija would bring him more food.

One day, at the top of the mountain, the Truth came to him!

An angel appeared before him and asked him to 'READ'. He replied, "I am not of those who can read!"

The Rasul of Allah (saw) explained, "Upon this reply, the angel held me and squeezed me so tightly that I thought I was going to collapse and then he let me go and again asked me to READ. Again

I told him, 'I am not of those who can read'. Upon this, he held me again and squeezed me so much that I didn't think I could handle it anymore, then he released me and again asked me to READ. Again I told him, 'I am not of those who can read'. Then he squeezed me for the third time and let me go and recited the verses, 'READ in the name of your Rabb who created you...'"

Upon this, the Rasul of Allah (saw) went home, his heart pounding. As soon as he saw Khadija he told her "Cover me, cover me!" When he settled down he explained what had happened to Khadija and told her he was scared.

Khadija said, "By Allah, Allah will never wrong you. You are kind to your relatives, patient during hardship, you work hard and help others to earn, you are generous to visitors and help the needy."

After this, she took him to her uncle Malikatul Nawfal. Nawfal, who was known as Waraqa during the time of ignorance, was a Christian... He knew how to write in Hebrew and wrote the Bible in Hebrew. However, he had now grown old and blind...

When Khadija took Muhammad (saw) to him she said, "My dearest uncle, listen to what your brother-in-law has to say..." Then the Rasul of Allah (saw) explained what he saw, upon this Waraqa said, "This is what Allah revealed to Moses! How I wish I had been young enough to be alive the day your people drive you out!"

The Rasul of Allah (saw) asked, "My people are going to drive me out?"

Waraqa answered, "Indeed, none has brought a message like yours who has not faced enmity and been driven out of his town. If I live until that day, I will surely help you..."

A short while after this incident another call came...

Again, it scared the Rasul of Allah (saw). He came to Khadija and said, "When I was in retreat I heard a call; I fear that it may be an order." Khadija said, "Nothing that comes to you from Allah should cause you fear. You protect the trusts, you're kind to your relatives, you are truthful..." and thus she comforted him.

Then Abu Bakr (ra) came. Khadija told Abu Bakr (ra) about what happened and asked him to take the Rasul to Waraqa. When the

Rasul of Allah (saw) came, Abu Bakr (ra) told him, "Let's go to Waraqa." "Who told you?" the Rasul asked. "Khadija" said Abu Bakr. Together, they went to Waraqa and explained what happened. The Rasul said, "When I go into retreat I hear a call 'O Muhammad,' which gives me fear and makes me flee."

Waraqa said, "Don't flee. When it comes, listen to it till the end until you understand what's been said. Then come and tell me what it tells you."

The next time the Rasul went into retreat he heard the call say:

"O Muhammad, say:

Bismillaahir-raḥmaanir-raḥeem

Al-ḥamduliLlaahi rabbil-`aalameen

Ar-raḥmaanir-raḥeem

Maalikiyawmid-deen

Iyyaakana`budu wa-iyyaakanasta`een

Ihdinaas-ṣiraaṭal-mustaqeem

Ṣiraaṭ alladheena-an`amta-`alayhim-ghayril-maghḍoobi`alayhim wa lad-ḍaalleen" after which "La ilaha illallah" was added.

When he told Waraqa about this, Waraqa said, "Good tidings to you! I witness that you are the one the son of Mary told about and you are upon a discipline like the discipline of Moses. You are a Nabi and you shall be charged with battle."

As can be seen, the first verse that was revealed to Muhammad was 'READ'. Almost all Islamic scholars are in agreement with this. The next revelation was the Basmalah and the Fatiha, seven verses that comprise the first chapter.

This being the case, what needs to be discerned is what exactly is meant by the command 'READ'!

If we take this as a classical form of literal reading, then he should have been given a text to read, yet he wasn't! No script of any form was given to him to read. So, how are we to understand this verse? Looking at it from a wide perspective and taking into consideration the conditions of the society then, their belief systems, thought patterns, etc., we may gain some insight into the situation.

As we know, there were 360 idols in the Kaaba back then, and people were generally polytheists. Some assumed gods on earth and some in heaven, they exalted and glorified them expecting their favor in return.

As a result of their dialogue with their imagined gods, they engaged in certain practices, such as sacrifices, offerings and ritualistic forms of beseeching and begging for certain benefits.

At that time, there was also a group of people who didn't believe in idols and deities, who didn't believe god was an entity in space, but that there was a limitless infinite conscious creative power that created the heavens and the earth. They were called '*Hanif*'. One of them was Abu Bakr (ra) and the other was Muhammad (saw).

Muhammad (saw) had figured there was no god in space, but he was still troubled by the inability to completely solve and grasp the essence of it. When this discomfort reached a serious point in his life, he left his business to his relatives, took a small amount of food with him and retreated to a cave and entered deep contemplation.

And then one day...

While Muhammad (saw) was heavily engaged in various meditative practices in the cave with the intention to reach the 'absolute reality' he encountered the extraordinary incident that changed his life.

Suddenly, an angel appeared before him, intensely squeezed him and commanded:

READ!

5

WHO ARE THE UNLETTERED?

Read what?

Muhammad (saw) couldn't read, because he was unlettered!

What did it mean to be unlettered?

Was it the inability to read a line of letters?

According to the Quran, the Arabs were of two kinds:

1.	The People of the Book; that is, those who were able to read and write the Old and New Testaments…

2.	The unlettered: those who couldn't read or write the Old and New Testament and thus couldn't take part in reproducing them through writing.

In other words, the division, according to the Quran, was done according to the ability to read and write the Old and New Testaments. Those who couldn't were called 'unlettered'.

There were some people who not only read the Old and New Testaments, but also assumed their reproduction through writing a duty… While others didn't read these books at all and worshipped various idols in the Kaaba.

A very small minority neither read/wrote these books nor worshipped idols; they were the Hanif.

Both Muhammad (saw) and Abu Bakr as-Siddiq (ra) were of the unlettered ones, i.e. they did not read and write the Old and New

Testaments as they were not of the People of the Book, and thus they were called Hanif.

This is the why the Quran addresses Muhammad (saw) with the verses:

"His Rasul, the Ummi (unlettered) **Nabi"**[1]

"Ask the People of the Book and the unlettered ones..."[2]

"And you did not recite any book (like the Torah and the Bible) **before** (the knowledge we disclosed)**, nor did you inscribe it with your right hand..."**[3]

If we look objectively, we will see that the verse "Ask the People of the Book and the unlettered ones" clearly divides the people into two categories: the lettered ones as the People of the Book, i.e. those who can read and write the Old and New Testaments, and the unlettered ones as those who can't read and write the Old and New Testaments.

The verse, "You teach the Book and the Wisdom even though you are of the unlettered ones" denotes, even though the Rasul did not read and write the Old and New Testaments, he taught people the knowledge contained in them; he informed them of past incidents recorded in these books. This proves he received news from the same source as these books, i.e. revelation, just as other Nabis did for the purpose of fulfilling their duty of *Nubuwwah*.

If he knew of and was able to narrate the information contained in the Old and New Testaments even though he was unlettered and thus hadn't read these books before, then this meant his source of

---

[1] Quran 7:158
[2] Quran 3:20
[3] Quran 29:48

information was that of Moses' and Jesus'. In other words, he was receiving divine revelation.

Another important distinction is in regards to the ability to read. What exactly did the word '*iqra*' (read) mean? Let's consider the place and conditions under which the command 'READ' was given to Muhammad (saw)… He was in front of a cave at the top of Mount Hira approximately 1,400 years ago and there was no written text in sight! Had there been and had Muhammad said, "I am not of those who can read," we would know doubtlessly this was literally about 'reading' as we know it. But, since this wasn't the case, and since, interestingly, Muhammad's (saw) response was, "I am not of those who can read" rather than "What shall I read?", which would have been the natural response of someone who didn't know what he was being asked to read, it's evident that Muhammad (saw) knew *what* he was being asked to read, yet he did not know *how* to! For his inability to read was not the inability to decipher a simple line of letters; it was not the inability to read and write in the literal sense!

So, what was it?

6

THE ABILITY TO READ

Until then, he didn't know how to read. Distressed by this inability, he retreated to the cave for months. Even this is interesting, for if this was about literal reading, why would he withdraw to a cave, when he could easily go to someone who could teach him how to read and write? Especially if we take into consideration the fact he was a merchant who had dealt with trade for so many years!

Taking things at a more surface value, certain people in the past deduced the Quran can only be a miracle if it was revealed through a Nabi who didn't know how to read and write. Thus, without going into any depth, in fact even blocking the path to certain truths, they decided an unlettered Nabi was one who did not know how to read and write. As if this elevated the Rasul of Allah or made him greater in some way! All of this is the result of not duly knowing the sublimity of the Rasul and not understanding the reality of what he brought forth.

According to many, a Nabi who emerged from the middle of the desert must not know how to read and write in order for the amazing new perspectives he introduced to be considered a miracle. As if the miraculous aspect of what he brought would be reduced in any way had he known how to read and write!

Let us not forget we are bound to believe that Muhammad (saw) was the Rasul and the final Nabi of Allah. Believing in his ability to read and write has nothing to do with the pillars of faith.

The only reason Muhammad (saw) was called unlettered was because he was not of the People of the Book; this is the external meaning of being unlettered. In other words, he was not a Jew or a Christian who then became a Nabi and brought a new religious understanding.

There is also a more hidden, in-depth meaning to the notion of being unlettered, which is far more important!

7

HANIF

Muhammad's (saw) distress due to his inability to read reached such an extent that for weeks he didn't want to see anyone, only wanting to be alone and reflect on this matter. None of the religions, belief systems, idols, etc., could answer the mass of questions that had accumulated in his head.

Neither Judaism, Christianity, the original format of which had been corrupted, nor idolatry meant anything to men like Muhammad (saw) and Abu Bakr (ra), even in those days. Therefore, they were automatically considered among the 'unlettered' ones, outside the scope of the 'People of the Book'.

But they were not of the idolaters either, which made them of the 'Hanif' group among the unlettered ones. The *Hanif* were those who were upon the path of Abraham; the path of Oneness.

According to our knowledge, Nabi Idris informed the people of the effects of celestial beings, i.e. astrology. Yet, when he made these explanations, he also knew that the administration of these powers was with the knowledge, will and power of Allah. After the science of astrology was exposed by Nabi Idris, those who were deprived of the ability to contemplate and discern the deeper truths became veiled from the primary power at the root of the system and got caught up with the stars and planets, accrediting all the power to them. This faulty judgment eventually led to assuming the existence of gods in space and thus the deification of celestial beings.

All teachings of all Nabis are subject to corruption and deformation in time, due to the narrow-minded ones who reduce and evaluate things according to their localized, rigid visions and conditioned concepts of right and wrong.

Astrology, a system and mechanism of Allah, was also misevaluated and in time it led to the deification and idolization of celestial beings. Eventually, idols were made in the names of these stars, and the Sun, the Moon and other planets were considered to be gods and thus worshipped.

At a time like this, a Nabi named Abraham emerged and, through deep introspection, he realized the Sun, the Moon and other stars could not be gods... When he came to this realization he said:

"Certainly, I have turned my face (my consciousness) **cleansed from the concept of a deity** (Hanif)**, toward the Fatir** (He who creates everything programmed according to its purpose) **who created the heavens and the earth, and I am not of the dualists."**[4]

The word face in this verse denotes consciousness, not the physical face. It is a reference to our inner face. For example, when we say someone is two-faced clearly we're not referring to their physical face, but to something about their character. Thus, the word face is used in reference to one's character here. We may even call it one's spiritual or intellectual face. It is simply a reference to one's consciousness.

Thus, when Abraham says 'my face' he is referring to his understanding:

I turn with my understanding, intellect, consciousness to One that is the Fatir of all that has been created in the heavens and the earth!

---

[4] Quran 6:79

8

THE RELIGION BASED ON NATURAL DISPOSITION

The Fatir?

Before defining this word, let us first remember two verses that elucidate the meanings of the words 'Hanif' and 'Fatir':

"Set your face (consciousness) **as a Hanif** (without the concept of a deity-god, without making shirq to Allah, i.e. with the consciousness of non-duality) **towards the One Religion** (the only system and order)**, the natural disposition** (fitrah) **of Allah** (i.e. the primary system and mechanism of the brain) **upon which Allah has created man. This is the infinitely valid system** (deen al-qayyim)**, but most people do not know."**[5]

Based on this verse, it is evident that 'Hanif' refers to the people of Abraham; those who are free from other religions and belief systems who turn only to Allah, that is, the people of Oneness.

Set your face as a Hanif towards the One Religion...

---

[5] Quran 30:30

To the natural disposition (fitrah) of Allah! That is, the religion that is best suitable to one's natural creation! Cling to that creation of Allah!

The religion of fitrah, the religion of Allah, the way of the Hanif are all Islam!

Religion is not to change one's natural disposition, it is to manifest the state of tranquility already inherent in one's natural creation. But most people don't know this, they seek religion not in their natural disposition, but in customs or they follow their desires...

Religion has two sources:

One is the natural disposition (fitrah) and the other is based on effort.

The natural disposition is completely divine; it is the guidance of the Reality! One based on personal effort, on the other hand, is more like an inspiration that arouses from various internal and external states and contemplations and can thus be subject to various infatuations, impairments and misjudgments, even leading to disbelief and duality...

The hadith "Everyone is born upon the natural disposition" is narrated by Abu Hurairah.

Anas (ra) also narrates, "Allah the Fatir has created everyone with a natural disposition such that they are all upon the religion of Allah"...

Natural disposition (fitrah) refers to the first creation; the first and original state of creation.

So, in this light let's consider the following:

Why is the word 'Fatir' used instead of 'Haliq,' which also means 'creator' or 'one who brings into existence'? Because when it comes to 'how' something is created, 'with which measure' and 'for which purpose', then 'Fatir' comes into play. Fatir is all about determining, planning, designing, measuring, timing, ordering, etc... All of these are what must be considered before bringing something into existence. Fatir designs creation to make it fulfill particular purposes. The 'religion of natural disposition' means the creational program that is automatically and unconditionally executed!

"Then established Himself in the heaven (to manifest some of His Names) **while it was in smoke form** (natural formless self) **and said to it** (consciousness) **and to the earth** (the body), **"Come willingly or by compulsion** (to manifest My Names)**!" They both said, "We come willingly to obey!"** (The heaven = intellectual state; and the earth = bodily organs. Both willingly manifest the qualities of the Names.)[6]

Considering that Allah is the Fatir of the heavens and the earth who created everything upon a 'natural disposition' then clearly it's impossible for them not to fulfill their creational purposes! The following verse also makes it evident that all things carry out the functions and actions necessitated by their natural disposition:

Say, "Everyone acts according to his own creation program (natural disposition; fitrah).**"**[7]

That is, Allah being the Fatir means that all beings, whether we think they are animated or unanimated, are all carrying out their natural creational programs and are thus in servitude... The biggest proof of this is the verse:

"Your Rabb has ordered you to serve only Him."[8]

Note that the verse says, 'Your Rabb has ordered'!

---

[6] Quran 41:11
[7] Quran 17:84
[8] Quran 17:23

Can the order of the Rabb change?

Let's remember the prayer of the Rasul (saw):

"O Allah, none can prevent what You ordain to give, and none can give what You ordain not to give. No such power exists that can refuse or change Your judgment."[9] (Hadith)

The order, determination, judgment of the Rabb is not subject to change! It will definitely be fulfilled!

"And to Him belongs whoever is in the heavens (conscious beings) **and the earth** (bodily beings). **Thus, all are in a state of devout obedience to Him** (in manifesting the qualities of His Names)..."[10]

If Allah has ordered that none is worshipped besides Him, which he has, then nothing, not a single unit of existence, can worship anything besides Him!

An eminent one in the past, one who has reached the essence, said:

"Because Allah has determined (kaza) that none be worshipped besides Him, He has created all things with His Names! Thus, whatever one may turn to in worship and servitude, he will always and inevitably be turning to Him!"

Thus, for whichever purpose the Fatir has programmed and created the heavens and the earth that is the purpose they will eventually fulfill – it is not possible for them not to!

---

[9] Sahih al-Bukhari Book 9 Vol 92 Hadith 395
[10] Quran 30:26

Now, let's go back to Abraham's conscious act of turning to Allah:

"Certainly, I have turned my face (my consciousness) **cleansed from the concept of a deity** (Hanif), **toward the Fatir** (He who creates everything programmed according to its purpose)**..."**[11]

That is to say, "I have realized there is nothing, no object that can be accepted as a god-deity that I can deify and idolize! Therefore, I have turned with my consciousness to the Fatir One who has designed and created the heavens and the earth as He likes and whose administration is upon them at every instance…"

"As a Hanif"![12]

That is, with the consciousness that there is no god in the heavens and the earth to worship! With the consciousness that idols and deities are unacceptable! With the realization there is an infinite and limitless force that creates and administers the whole of existence, the entire universe, the system and order at every instance as He likes and thus there is no external god beyond to be worshipped!

"And I am not of the dualists!"[13]

That is, I am not of those who assume the existence of deities besides Allah, the Wahid'ul Ahad! While Allah is the Absolute existence, I am not of those who conceive the existence of external gods and thus fall into duality! To assume the existence of a god besides Allah is to assume the existence of a being in space or to

---

[11] Quran 6:79
[12] Quran 6:79
[13] Quran 6:79

accept the deification of those who claim to be gods, such the Pharaoh, Namrud and the Antichrist (*dajjal*), etc.

9

ALLAH IS NOT COMPOSED OF PARTS

"But they attributed a portion of His servants to Him (denied His Absolute Oneness and assuming Him to be made up of parts, claimed He had a son)**... Indeed, man is clearly ungrateful!"**[14]

This verse highlights one of the most crucial truths in regards to the concept of the Oneness of 'Allah'.

Far from the teachings of Muhammad (saw) and unaware of the enormous difference between 'pantheism' and the 'Oneness' of Islam, some think Allah is a god externally present somewhere in space and that certain beings are 'parts' of Him or that Allah incarnates as people.

This misunderstanding is totally out of the failure to grasp the essence of the Quran.

The reality denoted by the verse above is clear:

Some ascribe 'portions' or 'parts' to Allah, yet Allah is far and free from this concept. This very idea goes against the reality denoted by the name Allah; it is invalid and unacceptable, because Allah is ONE. This Oneness is not a whole composed of parts. Because Allah is an infinite existence, an 'other' outside Allah is not possible; therefore, the idea of another 'part' or 'portion' is completely obsolete.

---

[14] Quran 43:15

We must understand this well, my friends...

If Allah was subject to space and locality, then we could claim at some point Allah ends and an 'other' begins, or that parts exist inside or outside Allah. But since Allah is a single whole and One (*Wahid'ul Ahad*), at least if this is what we believe, then it is only logical to deduce that the Oneness of Allah completely nullifies the idea of a 'part,' whether it be a part of Allah or outside of Allah!

Let us remember the verse:

"Say, 'Allah is Ahad (One)'**..."**[15]

More on this topic can be found in *Muhammad's Allah*. Let's now touch on another important topic...

---

[15] Quran 112:1

10

WHY ALLAH ISN'T A GOD

The word god is generally used in reference to a deity, typically one that is external, far and beyond.

The word Allah, on the other hand, is a name that references an infinite existence, one that is described with various qualities and attributes – though eventually all of them are descriptions in terms of the qualities they denote.

For example, the name Hulusi is a reference to me, it is my name. It cannot be translated into another language. Likewise, the name Allah is a name and thus cannot be translated into another language.

While words like 'god' evoke concepts of deities and godhood, the word Allah is a name that references a special existence and does not in any way denote godhood.

It is out of ignorance and lack of comprehension that people replace the word Allah with the word god.

Thus, when Allah is a name that references such an infinite existence that even the concept of an 'other' is not applicable, using words like 'god' not only suggests limitation, but also fragmentation and duality!

As the following verses warn:

"Do not form another god (in your head) **besides Allah!** **Otherwise** (as a result of your duality) **you will be degraded and isolated!"**[16]

"Do not turn to (assume the existence of) **a god** (exterior manifestations of power or your illusory self) **besides Allah. For there is no god, only HU! Everything** (in respect of its 'thing'ness) **is inexistent, only the face of HU** (only that which pertains to the Absolute Reality) **exists!"**[17]

That is, when Allah is the All-encompassing Absolute Existence whose presence is in every iota of the perceivable and unperceivable worlds, do not fall into ignorance and assume Allah is a deity that exists far and beyond you! For this kind of projection will only lead you away from the reality of Allah and to deification and duality!

As a result, you will become deprived of the reality of 'unity' in the Quran, and thus commit the greatest wrong to yourself!

"Assuredly, duality is a great wrongdoing!"[18]

---

[16] Quran 17:22
[17] Quran 28:88
[18] Quran 31:13

11

HOW CLOSELY CAN A NAME DEFINE THE ONE THAT IS NAMED?

Here I'd like to draw your attention to another important point…

A name is a reference to something; we use names as tags when we want to talk about or ponder on a particular thing.

As known, the word Allah is a name. Just as my name, Hulusi, doesn't reveal anything about my character, so too the name Allah does not in any way reveal anything about the infinite existence referenced by it.

If one was to hear the word Allah for the first time, they might only know it is the name of a being, but they won't in any way be informed about what kind of being it references, whether Allah is a god or something else…

When the Rasul (saw) told us about Allah he laid emphasis on the truth that it was not a reference to a god or a deity. When he said "your god is Allah," he said this to clarify the fact that what we think and assume to be god is actually Allah.

To say "your god is Allah" does not in any way mean Allah is a god. On the contrary, it denotes the following:

"That which you think is god doesn't exist, it isn't real. There is no deity-god, there is only Allah. Thus, what you assume to be god is also Allah in disguise. The reality denoted by the word 'Allah', in terms of His qualities, has nothing to do with your assumed god. So, abandon your idea of an external deity-god and try to discern the reality denoted by the name Allah!"

Take a few minutes to ponder on the subject of the Earth and the Sun, which is 1,303,000 times greater than the Earth, and the 400 billion stars like the Sun comprising our galaxy and the billions of such galaxies comprising the universe that we perceive, and the innumerous universes within each other... And then a single point from which a single angle is projected, an angle within which all of the above is created... A single point, a single instance!

But there are infinite instances, points and angles that are formed by these points, and thus infinite universes within universes in the sight of the One called Allah!

Whatever a totem of one of the tribes in Africa means in the sight of the universe, that's what people's deity-god is in the sight of Allah!

How distant is the concept of "god" in today's society to the infinite existence named Allah that Muhammad (saw) explained through the Quran?

The Quran has come for 'humans', those who have cleansed themselves from the filth of godhood and duality, who use their brain to contemplate so they may discern the reality of the One named Allah and shape their lives accordingly!

Earthlings, on the other hand, will continue to be herded like all other creatures on the Earth!

Indeed, Muhammad (saw) was free from the idea of god and duality, yet he still continued searching for the truth...

12

THE FIRST REVELATIONS

As a Hanif, Muhammad (saw) did not believe in external gods or idols, his endeavor was to understand Allah and fulfill his servitude to him.

How did existence, the world, this system come about? How did it function?

Either it had to be the work of consciousness, whereby everything was consciously formed with a system and order, or it had to be the result of blind chance, which could only result in chaos!

If we assume everything in the heavens and the earth is operating within a conscious system, then it follows there must be a conscious Being who has made it so.

But, who or what is this Being?

Does it have a place?

What was its relation to existence?

How was it related to the notion of 'I'?

Was it possible to reach this sublime Being?

If so, how?

These were the kind of questions Muhammad (saw) was asking, and the longer it was taking to find the answers, the more he was feeling uneasy and unable to rest, until one day he encountered something he was not expecting.

An angel of extraordinary dimensions named Gabriel at the top of Mount Hira squeezed him tightly and called out:

'READ'!

Muhammad (saw) did not ask, "What shall I read?" For he knew what he was being asked to read! His problem was he didn't know how to read it! That's why he retreated to the cave in the first place!

So, he replied:

"I am not of those who can read! I can't read!"

Upon this Gabriel squeezed him again and repeated:

"READ!"

But helplessly, Muhammad (saw) still couldn't read, so again he replied:

"I am not of those who can read"

Finally Gabriel squeezed him for the third time and then said:

1. READ with the Name of your Rabb (with the knowledge that comprises your being) **who created.**

2. Created man from alaq (a clot of blood; genetic composition).

3. READ! For your Rabb is Akram (most generous).

4. Who taught (programmed the genes and the essential qualities) **by the Pen.**

5. Taught man that which he knew not.

Let's also remember the verse:

"And He taught (programmed) **Adam** (the name 'Adam' in the Quran references every single human, who in reality is nonexistent and has been created from a state of nothingness through the manifestation of a composition of Names) **all of the Names** (all knowledge pertaining to the Names and their manifestation)."[19]

How are these verses related?

Both of these verses are about the creation of man and the sublime quality given to him during his creation.

So, going back to our topic, what exactly was Muhammad (saw) being asked to read by the 'angel'?

Considering that Muhammad was a Hanif who was trying to decipher the system in which he was living and his ability to read was activated via the revelation of the angel, the quality and force that was activated was already inherent within him, it just wasn't active; he hadn't yet used it.

When he told the angel he could not read, the angel 'squeezed' him, which brings us to the other important point.

Why did Gabriel squeeze him? Gabriel isn't like us, he isn't made of matter, i.e. he does not have a physical body, so clearly this isn't a physical act of squeezing. Angels are ethereal; they are comprised of light, while the jinn are made of a type of fire. Neither have physical bodies like we do. Their effect on humans is via the electromagnetic impulses they send to the human brain.

Indeed, the human brain is constantly subject to the effects of angels and jinn.

---

[19] Quran 2:31

13

ANGELS AND THE SPIRIT

The human spirit is formed in the body!

Imam Ghazali also explains the human spirit is formed after the formation of the body in the mother's womb, and the idea of spirits being created earlier and then sent to earth gradually is nonsense:

Based on the teachings of the Rasul of Allah (saw) and as Ghazali explains in his book Rawzatu't Talibeen, the spirit-body is inexistent before the biological body is formed.

Spirits are not created elsewhere and then sent to the bodies as they come to earth, this idea is totally incorrect. This view goes back earlier than Islam, to certain Buddhist philosophies. To keep the poverty stricken people away from rebellion, they were made to believe they will be rewarded with wealth and the chance to come back to earth with a better body and better living conditions if they were to consent to their current state and be patient… After which, various ideas of reincarnation were introduced, i.e. that one can come back to earth with a new body after death…

According to Islam, this idea is a complete fabrication and absolutely invalid.

Reincarnation is advocated by those who engage in necromancy and who claim they are the reincarnated body of Rumi or other scholars and saints, or sadly, by those who have become possessed by jinn.

Angels and the Spirit

In 1972, I explained in my book *Spirit Man Jinn* what the spirit is, how it's formed and why reincarnation isn't possible. More information can be obtained from there, for now I'll only a share a few points.

The spirit of each person is formed by the brain in the mother's womb as a result of certain cosmic effects, and at the time of death, it departs from the body and continues its life in its own dimension.

"When death comes to one of them, he says, "My Rabb, send me back (to the worldly life) **so that I might do righteousness in that which I left behind** (i.e. a faithful life that I did not heed or give importance to; the potential that I did not utilize and activate).**" No!** (It is impossible to go back!) **His words are invalid!** (His request is unrecognized in the system) **and behind them is a barrier** (an isthmus; a difference of dimension) **until the Day they are resurrected** (they cannot go back; reincarnation, being re-born for another worldly life, is not possible!).**"**[20]

"None shall be brought back after death" (Hadith)

The verses and hadith make it evident there is no return to the worldly life after experiencing death.

The Rasul of Allah (saw), in terms of being Allah's vicegerent (caliphate), was already determined in the knowledge of Allah as the composition and manifestation of Allah's names, before Adam was created.

That is, Rasulullah (saw), the caliphate of Allah, was the first created meaning in Allah's knowledge, though he was the last Nabi that became manifest on earth. The reality of Muhammad (saw) was first created in a perfect fashion in Allah's knowledge, then Adam was formed from earth. Earth denotes the human body, that we perceive with our five senses and its water and mineral-based makeup.

---

[20] Quran 23:99-100

This earthly makeup, comprised of water and minerals, works like a bioelectric factory; it converts the liquid and solid input into bioelectric energy and sends it to the brain. The brain works like a microcomputer; it receives the bioelectric energy and converts its data into a radial type of energy, which forms the holographic body called 'spirit' and also radiates this energy to its surroundings.

14

THE UNIVERSE PERCEIVED BY THE BRAIN

What is a 'meaning' and how is it formed?

We must first understand well that nobody perceives the universe as it actually is. When one talks about the universe, they are actually referring to their 'personalized' universe, a relative world they perceive with their five senses.

The universe begins as pure energy and expands to infinite dimensions with its infinite wavelengths. Each of these wavelengths denotes a meaning. We may either say each wavelength is meaningful or that 'meanings' have been called 'wavelengths'…

There are multiple universes all within each other, perceivable in their own dimension, yet an 'unknown' to others. The universe we all perceive with our common makeup is the universe of humans.

The universe of what is commonly referred to as 'aliens' in our day or in religious terminology the 'jinn' or 'satan' is also different.

Yet all of these different universes are based on our very limited five senses.

Science is unfortunately advancing in the wrong direction today. Rather than exploring the vastness of the universe, if they were to put their efforts into exploring the different wavelengths comprising the universes and developing tools for this purpose its benefit to mankind will be unfathomable.

If we can truly comprehend the fact that everything in the universe is made of these wavelengths, we will inevitably come to the realization that everything we perceive and not perceive in the universe is conscious, alive and meaningful.

"There is nothing that does not exalt (tasbih) **Him with hamd** (evaluation of the corporeal worlds created with His Names, as He wills)**! But you do not perceive their functions!"**[21]

In religious terminology, the conscious beings in these layers of existence have been termed 'angels' and the universal meanings and concepts have been referred to as the Names of Allah.

Everything that exists within all the multiple universes is nothing other than the perception of groups of meanings forming the universe in which they reside. In this sense, the meanings referred to as 'angels' carry out multiple functions based on the meanings they compose.

Thus, the angel Gabriel is a highly conscious being comprised of meanings such as *Aleem, Basir, Fattah, Hakeem* and *Muhyi*.

His function is to activate and open the chosen ones via the act of 'squeezing' and informing them of Allah's universal system and values so they may be a guide to the people.

---

[21] Quran 17:44

15

WHY DID GABRIEL SQUEEZE?

What is the meaning of Gabriel's act of squeezing Muhammad (saw)?

I had previously talked about how most religious explanations are metaphoric. Let's see how the metaphor of 'squeezing' has been used with an example:

The Rasul of Allah (saw) says the following in regards to the state of the deceased in the grave:

"The grave squeezed him so much that his ribs were nearly going to intertwine... His agony reached the Throne, but man did not hear..."

The squeezing mentioned here is obviously not a physical squeezing of dirt and soil, but something totally different. It's difficult to explain its meaning even today, let alone in those days...

But with the aid of Allah, I will try to explain to the best of my knowledge, as my purpose of creation is to clarify as much as possible the matters of religion.

As I explained in detail in the *Mystery of Man*, the human brain is programmed by radial beings of very high frequencies called 'angels' who are comprised of nur (light), thereby becoming able to manifest the Names of Allah as certain formulas.

Genetic data that we inherit is activated and expressed according to the capacity we've obtained through cosmic means enabling us with the mental skills with which we live.

Each brain cell is programmed with certain frequencies that carry specific meanings and thus gains new insights or leads to the expression of certain genetic data...

Actually, every thought we have, whether we express it or not, is a composition of the concepts referenced by the Names of Allah, which forms as a result of genetic and cosmic, i.e. angelic, effects!

Just as 'mankind' is comprised entirely of compositions of Names, so is the whole of existence; all that we perceive and all that we are unable to perceive, including the angels.

In this light, Gabriel is a Name composition that programs the brains of certain chosen individuals, due to the Names that are dominant in their makeup, enabling them to READ. That is, when Gabriel squeezed Muhammad (saw), he sent impulses of certain frequencies to his brain, such as *Aleem, Basir, Hakeem, Fattah, Muhyi*, etc., and thus instigated their manifestation. Essentially, these Names were already present in his makeup by birth, but their ratio in his composition weren't sufficient to activate the Nabi quality. With the intervention of Gabriel, the ratio of these Names in his brain was increased to a capacity sufficient to manifest the message of the final Nabi.

This grand brain experience could only be defined by a person as the act of constricting, squeezing or tightening. So it was after this act of squeezing, the new insights resulting from the impulses sent to his brain, that Muhammad began to READ.

1. READ with the Name of your Rabb (with the knowledge that comprises your being) **who created.**

2. Created man from alaq (a clot of blood; genetic composition).

3. READ! For your Rabb is Akram (most generous).

4. Who taught (programmed the genes and the essential qualities) **by the Pen.**

5. Taught man that which he knew not.

What does 'Pen' mean?

If reading isn't about literal reading, then what does this Pen symbolize?

Renowned Fahraddin Razi says the Pen is the intellect. The Rasul of Allah (saw) points to this with the hadith:

"Let it be known that Allah first created the Pen and commanded it, 'Write!' The Pen asked, 'What shall I write my Rabb?' He said, 'Write the destiny' … And the Pen wrote everything that happened and everything that shall happen…"

The Pen symbolizes the Perfect Man according to the Sufi intimates of reality. They call the intellect of the Perfect Man 'the First Intellect' and his spirit the 'Spirit of Muhammad'… *The Reality of Muhammad* also points to this truth…

Let's also remember the verse:

Say, "Nothing will befall us except what Allah has prescribed for us!"[22]

Though it's the Pen that writes, Allah attributes it to Himself, for the Pen exists with the existence of Allah… Just like the verse **"And you threw not** (the arrow) **when you** (illusory self; ego) **threw, but it was Allah who threw!"**[23]

The unity of existence is based on such verses.

---

[22] Quran 9:51
[23] Quran 8:17

In modern terms, the Pen that determines everything that has happened and shall happen can be called the cosmic consciousness. That is, the manifestation of the attribute of knowledge or pure consciousness!

This is what 'taught man what he knew not':

"And He taught (programmed) **Adam** (the name 'Adam' in the Quran references every single human, who in reality is nonexistent and has been created from a state of nothingness through the manifestation of a composition of Names) **all of the Names** (all knowledge pertaining to the Names and their manifestation). **Then said to the angels, 'Explain the** (qualities of the) **Names of** (Adam's) **existence, if you insist on your claim.'"**

No doubt, teaching Adam the Names is a reference to Adam manifesting the Names of Allah. However, all of these Names are present in man's creation as a composition, some of which are more dominant and some of which are less... The expression "*BismiRabbik*" (in the name of the Rabb, the Names that comprise one's essence) refers to the presence of these Names in one's makeup.

16

WHY A CLOT OF BLOOD?

One may ask, "The above verses are in regard to knowledge and power endowed in one's essence to enable their ability to read... This being the case, how is man's creation 'from a clot of blood' related with this topic?"

In the first chapter I talked about man being a composition of divine Names, in the second chapter I covered the word 'alaq' and the transfer of this supremacy from one person to another through genetic data...

Though the word 'alaq' is generally translated as a clot of blood, it's more correct to consider it as a group of developing cells containing all of the genetic data, for it is the meaning denoted by that word that matters!

If we evaluate the above verses in this light, the first five verses can be understood as:

Read! You were created to comprise the meanings referenced by the name of your Rabb and this supremacy pertaining to the dimension of meanings reaches you through genetic inheritance.

Read! Your Rabb is *Akram*. That is, he possesses an infinite wealth of meanings, and because of this, he has encoded these meanings in your brain with the cosmic pen... He manifests what man knows not in man's makeup...

At this point, one may ask:

The word '*allamal*' (taught) has always been translated as 'to teach,' how is it that you construe this as 'programming one's makeup' or 'manifesting through one's constitution'?

It's quite simple... Let's remember the verse:

"And He taught (programmed) **Adam** (the name 'Adam' in the Quran references every single human, who in reality is nonexistent and has been created from a state of nothingness through the manifestation of a composition of Names) **all of the Names** (all knowledge pertaining to the Names and their manifestation)."[24]

This verse talks about the first creation of Adam, the point at which Adam has not yet become conscious... It is after this act of teaching Allah's Names, (Adam being created in a way to manifest Allah's Names) that consciousness comes about!

That is, the primary factor that enabled consciousness to Adam was the meanings of the Names of Allah endowed in his being during his creation. As a result of this endowment, Adam commenced his life as a conscious being or '*nefsi natik*' on earth...

This is why it's almost as if Gabriel is saying to Muhammad (saw):

"You are an individual of the human kind who has been created with the Names of Allah (the meanings pertaining to them). The supremacy of the Names has been transmitted to you through genetic means.

The brain has the quality and capability to understand these meanings, and to read the system and order of Allah. So, read! You've been taught all of the meanings of the Names to inform you of what you don't know, i.e. your brain has been programmed with it.

---

[24] Quran 2:31

This programming has been done with the cosmic pen, i.e. angelic force. As a result of this, you know what you didn't previously know and you can read what you previously couldn't read!"

The '*nur*' (light of knowledge) was sent to Muhammad's brain by Gabriel, who is also a *nur*-based makeup, or in today's language, the impulses sent to Muhammad's brain by the radial being called Gabriel created a great sense of pressure in him and, as a result of this, the capacity that was activated in his brain manifested the supremacy of *Nubuwwah*…

Notice that I use the word 'manifest' rather than saying it simply 'happened'.

For, if the person doesn't have this capacity by birth, influences that come later cannot activate the *Nubuwwah* capacity… Practices done later or skills that are acquired later cannot manifest the supremacy of sainthood (*wilayah*)…

Another important point to consider is: From which level or state to read?

The word used in the above verse, '*BismiRab*' inevitably brings us to this point. As can be seen, the verse says in the name of your Rabb rather than Allah or Rahman… Since the Quran is the 'word of Allah' and thus it's Hakeem, it follows that every word in the Quran has been used based on a wisdom, specifically selected to denote the meaning that is intended.

Unfortunately, however, most Quran translations do not heed this fine point and words that are far from the original have been used leading to different meanings…

The biggest example of this is the verse:

"And serve your Rabb until there comes to you *yakeen*"[25]

If we look at other translations the word *yakeen* in this verse has generally been translated as death. Whereas, if death was intended

---

[25] Quran 15:99

the word '*mawt*' would have been used instead. Generally, the word *mawt* is used to denote death! Death is only one type of certainty.[26]

If we really want to understand the Quran and attain the deeper meanings in it, we must definitely understand the words that have been used and why those specific words have been chosen for those verses instead of others.

---

[26] More information can be found on the meaning of the word yakeen in *Gavsiye Aciklamasi (Turkish)*

17

WHY IN THE NAME OF THE RABB?

The reason why 'in the name of your Rabb' comes immediately after the command 'READ' signifies that this 'reading' needs to be done with the supremacy of the compositional qualities denoted by the Names comprising existence (*Rububiyyah*).

That is, the kind of reading that's required isn't from the level of *Uluhiyyah* or *Rahmaniyyah* (the quantum potential), but from the level of *Rububiyyah*.

If it said 'Bismillah' after saying 'read,' then it would have necessitated the reading happens from the level of *Uluhiyyah*. Whereas, because the supremacy of *Uluhiyyah* encompasses the Absolute Essence (*dhat*), it's impossible to read from this level.

The Rasul of Allah (saw) says, "Do not contemplate upon the Absolute Essence (*dhat*) of Allah!" to indicate this truth.

It's not possible to read from the level of *Rahmaniyyah* either, for this is the level at which the Sublime Essence knows Himself with all of His attributes; man's capacity is insufficient to do so.

As Muhammad (saw) used to pray during the night (*tahajjud*):

"It's not possible for me to evaluate and praise You the way You know and evaluate Your self!"

One may ask:

Based on the truth, 'Rahman created Adam upon his own image,' if man has been created upon the reality of Rahman, then why can't man read upon *Rahmaniyyah*?

It's quite natural for Rahman to have created Adam upon His own image because there is no other existence besides Himself upon which He can create Adam! Obviously, He's going to create him upon His own attributes!

But, let us not forget that man is essentially a hominid who has been given the good news of being created with the Names of Allah, and thus with grace.

Indeed, His grace has succeeded His wrath!

All states that man has encountered or is to encounter, even if it seems contradictory to him and gives him pain, is upon grace, including the state of hell.

However, the fact that he's created with grace and upon the Rahman reality does not necessarily mean that a 'hominid' or 'human' can read upon *Rahmaniyyah*...

For, though he may be created upon the reality of Rahman, his manifestation is at the level of *Rububiyyah* as an individual composition of the Names in the dimension of multiplicity...

The dimension of *Rububiyyah* is the level at which the meanings of the Names of Allah become manifest as infinite compositions... The world of acts (*af'al*), which comprises the world of forms, including the jinn, angels and humans, derives its existence from the level of *Rububiyyah*...

The level of *Rububiyyah* is the level where the Rabbani forces are activated and differentiated from one another. This is the dimension of multiplicity...

It is the area under the Throne!

The area above the Throne is completely abstract, the dimension of *Jabarut*!

We can also call the dimensional area under the Throne 'universe' in the absolute sense, not the universe of humans we talk about today!

All countless living conscious beings outside our perception can be categorized generally as humans, jinn and angels.

But what is of concern to us is the first and the third…

Why are angels important?

Notice that *Amantu* begins with "Amantu billahi wa malaikatuhu"… Why is faith in angels mentioned before faith in the Book and the Rasul?

The essence and origin of every object comprising the universe is angelic.

Everything that is perceivable and unperceivable to us in the universe is formed with this angelic fabric. They are '*Nur*' or compositions of Names. Thus, they're conscious and powerful as necessitated by their form and dimension.

Everything that exists in the universe is a composition of consciousness + energy.

These innumerous beings called angels comprising the universe and all qualities pertaining to them composes the dimension we call the world of acts…

The primary source of power that drives all actions in this dimension is no other than the qualities pertaining to the supremacy of *Rububiyyah*…

This being the case, one can only read the universal system that manifests these infinite meanings depending on the Rabbani capacity of the person, which is again activated by the Rabbani power of the person.

Muhammad (saw) got to know the system and order of his Rabb by reading the book of the universal system with the power that was revealed to him, as he was asked to.

This act of reading terrified him, he was awed by what he read and thus he felt the need to cover what he knew, so he covered himself… But after a period of internalizing these truths, he had to share it with the people:

"O wrapped one (*Muddathir*); arise and warn![27]

And thus he began to warn the people...

I guess by now it has become evident that reading has nothing to do with our classical understanding of literal reading...

To READ is to read the secrets of the universal book of the system comprising the qualities of the dimension of *Rububiyyah* with insight, foresight and introspection!

18

THE MISCONCEPTION OF HEAVENLY RELIGIONS

As we all know,

"Indeed, the religion (system and order) **in the sight of Allah is Islam!"**[28]

"And whoever seeks a religion (system and order) **other than Islam** (the consciousness of being in a state of submission) **his search will be ineffective!"**[29]

Since all Nabis from Adam to Muhammad (saw) have taught Islam – the only religion in the sight of Allah – the plural term 'religions' is incorrect.

There is either a single religion defined by Allah or many belief systems resulting from the theorization of human thought.

It is a greater mistake to assume there are many religions and then to divide them into categories, such as heavenly and not-heavenly, as if there are a few heavenly religions. This is totally from ignorance.

---

[28] Quran 3:19
[29] Quran 3:85

Even the term heavenly religion is an incorrect statement in terms of where it leads people.

The religion of Islam? Heavenly religion? Or the religion of Allah?

The term heavenly religion comes from the time of idol worshippers to denote a god 'other than the gods on earth' since heavenly denotes the sky!

As soon as you say 'heaven' or 'sky' you've defined a location. Whereas, the religion of Islam does not in any way make a reference to a place in the heavens.

Allah is not a god in space; He does not have a location. The Quran is the word of Allah, not a book from space! Even Gabriel did not descend from a star or a planet in the heavens!

"And indeed, it is HU who is the Rabb of Sirius (the star)!"[30]

This verse evidences that the star Sirius is not a god and Allah is free from the concept of a location.

The One referenced by the name 'Allah' is an infinite and sublime being and the Quran is His word, it has been revealed by Him, i.e. from a dimensional depth, and thus it is the universal book of Allah!

To say Islam, the religion in the sight of Allah, is a cosmic religion is equally a sign of ignorance!

Religion belongs neither to space nor to dimensions, nor is it based on a universe-based concept.

Religion is from Allah, it belongs to Allah! Allah is the owner, definer, maintainer and protector of religion.

Expressions such as 'cosmic religion' are uttered out of ignorance.

---

[30] Quran 53:49

Our job is to serve in the path of explaining and clarifying the religion of Islam in the light of science and modern knowledge to reveal its depth. If my works are taken as an imposition of a new religion, this can only be a sign of ignorance and lack of insight.

The term 'cosmic religion' denotes the system comprising the universe, which eventually leads away from Islam to pantheism.

Expressions such as 'cosmic existence' or 'cosmic consciousness' can't be used in reference to Allah either.

Just as the word heavenly connotes a location and hence can't be used to describe 'the religion in the sight of Allah,' the word cosmic is a dimensional concept and hence can't be used in reference to Allah.

The revelation of the Divine word or the descent of Gabriel or other angels to humans is not location-based, but dimension-based and hence the expression 'cosmic being' can be used in reference to Gabriel and other angels.

We can call the universe that we perceive and even the absolute universe that displays the compositional Names of Allah a 'cosmic book' or the 'universal book' or the 'book of the system'… In fact, we can even say the command READ is to read the Names of Allah with insight, foresight and introspection, which manifests itself as the universal system or book.

It's all about the universal book being read by a human being, a hominid!

In other words, a hominid is becoming aware of, comprehending and evaluating the universal system.

We don't expect these concepts to be understood immediately by those who have been conditioned with a classical approach to religion; comprehension requires time…

In time, my works will be first denied and rejected, then argued over and then, once an objective and unprejudiced approach is taken, they will be confirmed.

But this does not apply to everyone, of course…

Allah will surely enable those who approach my works with sincerity, without judgment and prejudice to see the truths due to their sincerity.

We've covered what READing is about and how it's done... Now let's move on to the next point...

19

HOW TO READ THE SYSTEM

How can the system be read?

With the power and consciousness of your Rabb comprising your essence; that is, by evaluating the dimension perceived by the five senses with insight, foresight and introspection. With the revelation by the angel who reads the Preserved Tablet (*lawh al-mahfuz*)

As I tried to explain previously, terms such as 'religion', 'Quran' and 'Gabriel' have not descended from a god in a specific location in space somewhere... As the concept of dimensions was not known to the people in past centuries, it has been narrated as though things took place in the heavens...

Let's consider an experience the Rasul (saw) had one day as he was praying, he saw heaven and hell... While the things he saw in paradise attracted him and incited him to reach out to them, the things he saw in hell repelled him and made him want to step back...

As can be seen, such experiences are not confined to specific locations in space or on earth, but are altogether relative and thus in higher or lower dimensions according to our perception.

Things that are perceived and seen outside the scope of what everyone else perceives and sees are visions pertaining to other dimensions.[31]

---

[31] Refer to *The Observing One* chapter 'Higher matter' for more information.

The primary and biggest reason why religion isn't duly appraised today is because of the language barrier or the inability to understand the terms and concepts that are employed.

But if we realize that religion is disclosed from a dimension not a location, we can stop looking for god in space and understand the reality of Allah, angels, jinn, the life of this world and beyond.

This is why we must understand the concept of dimensions well before we move on to the topics of *lawh al-mahfuz*, Gabriel and what's been read.

20

DIMENSIONS

According to traditional narrations, there are seven levels between the Earth and the orbital area of the Moon. This makes our current place of residence seven layers underground.

That is, the layer above us is the sixth, the one above that is the fifth and so on until the Moon. This narration actually defines the layers of Earth's atmosphere.

Beyond the atmosphere of the earth, the first heaven (in the sky) is where the Moon is, the second is the orbital area of Mercury, the third corresponds to Venus, the fourth to the Sun, the fifth to Mars, the sixth to Jupiter and the seventh to Saturn.

Then comes the galaxies and the Milky Way, generally known as the Throne (*Qursi*)…

Beyond the solar system, the concept of locality extends to the galactic level…

All other concepts and beings defined in religion are beyond the scope of locality on the dimensional basis!

Essentially, the word 'cosmic' denotes dimensionality not to reference a location in the universe or a concept pertaining to the universe.

Cosmic rays are not in regards to rays coming from space, but to the waves emitted by the beings in the dimensional depths in space, i.e. rays pertaining to the lower dimensions. Hence, the term 'cosmic beings' does not reference aliens or the jinn, but beings that live in the levels outside our dimension, known in religious terms as angels.

What does dimensional mean?

We only perceive an extremely limited section from an infinite array of existence as our material world based on our five senses. Our knowledge of life forms in our world compared to those outside our solar system is like a drop in the ocean!

Life forms within our solar system and our scope of perception is 'nothing' in respect to one higher or one lower dimension.

The Rasul of Allah (saw) says:

"Everything in the first heaven compared to the second is like a ring in the desert, and everything in the second heaven compared to the third is also like a ring in the desert, and so on until the 7th heaven."

This hadith points to our place in the universe among infinite layers of existence...

If you recall, after Gabriel squeezed, Muhammad (saw) was able to perceive other dimensions and their beings.

All gnostics and intimates of reality mutually agree that the word 'heavens' in religious texts actually refers to the stars within the galaxies, but this can only be discerned if the concept of 'dimensions' is correctly understood.

All perceived paradises and their life forms are not on the physical structure of these stars, but within their dimensional depths...

Even the fact that hell is the Sun is not in terms of its physical structure, but in respect to the lower dimension in which past spirits and the jinn reside.

The perceiving of hell and its tenants by the people of hell while in their graves, as established through various hadith, is also due to perceiving the Sun from the realm of the spirit.

Surely, before us, countless enlightened ones have observed these realities, which we've had the privilege to observe as the bounty (*lutuf*) of Allah.

However, because the concept of dimensions was not known in the past, their observations and interactions with the other dimensions have been narrated symbolically and thus conceived as though it took place somewhere in space.

My advice to someone who wants to develop himself is, "Even if you don't understand, at least don't deny!"

Just as we can't perceive the jinn, the martyrs or the spirits of saints around us even though they share our world with us, we are unable to perceive the paradises and their life forms on other stars because they are in other dimensions within those stars, yet out of ignorance and prejudgment we deny their existence altogether. The same thing applies to the Sun, which in reality is hell.

Having explained the concept of 'worlds' as the different dimensions of existence, let us now move on to the topic of '*lawhi mahfuz*' and 'angels'…

From the dimension of pure consciousness, which encompasses the meaning denoted by the word 'energy', to the dimension of what we perceive to be matter and even higher matter, every dimension has a unique structure and conscious life forms…

Every segment of existence, from the micro cosmos to the macro cosmos is a conscious segment of life, and each of them is perceived by its own life forms and those of one higher dimension.

Lawh al-mahfuz is the dimension of divine decree and fate pertaining to the Name compositions that constitute the world of multiplicity. It is the level of knowledge and consciousness; the manifestation of Allah's knowledge and ruling in the world of acts.

Everything that pertains to the world of multiplicity has been formed by the particulars of this level.

Nothing that is recorded and inscribed here is subject to change!

The source of creation of all angels and life forms in the dimensions beneath us and up to us is derived from here.

Here, we are present as knowledge; our design and program is determined at this level. Everything from pre-eternity to post-eternity is present as knowledge here.

As for Gabriel...

Since Allah isn't a god in space who sends orders and commands, everything in the universe is formed through causality.

If we perceive the cause, rather than the 'causer of the cause,' we will inevitably accredit the seeming cause and claim, "it was because of this thing, or that person" rather than saying, "It was Allah who gave and Allah who took"...

"Allah is free (*ghani*) from the worlds." That is, Allah is free from 'doing' and 'causing', all such expressions are metaphoric! Yet, on the other hand, no matter which name is used, the one is who is named is always one of His Name compositions. Thus, every action resulting from every unit of existence is tied to him via a rope of wisdom, as there is nothing else in existence other than Him!

In this light, the essence of the angel Gabriel is no other than the One, his meaning is a Name composition and his structure is '*nur*' or energy!

Because he's a conscious energy being, he can choose to appear in any form he desires depending on the meaning he wants to transmit to the person via radial impulses.

All but one form of Gabriel's appearances are those that he wants perceived. In terms of his origin, he's an abstract being free of a form.

As such, the angel Michael, responsible for the distribution of sustenance, and Azrael, responsible for death and transformation, and Ishmael, whose task is in regards to the angels who are formed by the deeds of the people, are all comprised of '*nur*', they are power + consciousness beings. They all fulfill their duties via reading the *lawh al-mahfuz*.

Gabriel, whose job is to direct those who are chosen as Nabi, has read the *lawh al-mahfuz* once and then notified Muhammad (saw) gradually.

How did notification begin and why?

Notification commenced with the first verses of the chapter *Alaq* and the experience of squeezing... But why was this necessary? Why did Gabriel squeeze Muhammad (saw)?

21

RECOGNIZING MUHAMMAD (SAW)

Some, who are veiled from the reality, indecently claim:

"Muhammad was an honest and smart man, so with the permission of Allah Gabriel gave him the duty of prophethood and thus he lived according to Gabriel's instructions. He was merely Allah's deliveryman! There's no reason to overly exalt Muhammad (saw), the Sufis exalt him more than necessary and give him more credit than needed. He lived like a simple man, his only difference was that he delivered the commands of Allah to people as per Gabriel's instructions! All the great saints and masters including Hadhrat Ali, Abu Bakr, Naqshibandi, Aldulqadir al-Jilani, Imam Ghazali and Ibrahim Erzurumi are all exaggerating the importance of Muhammad and his words! The Quran is sufficient for us, there's no need to heed the hadith so much, most of it is fabrication anyway!.." and so on…

A 'deliverer' is one who carries something from one place to another without really knowing what he's carrying. To call the Rasul of Allah (saw) a deliveryman is to claim he's unconscious of his duty!

One who claims such a thing can only do so out of not knowing the supremacy and depth of Muhammad (saw), which leads such people to deny even authentic hadith. Whereas, hadith are like the poles upon which the throne of the Quran rests! They teach us how the verses of the Quran need to be understood and evaluated.

It was the Rasul of Allah (saw) who taught us, in the light of the Quran, how Islam is to be lived; the truth has reached us today via his explanations and teachings.

The religion of Islam consists of the Quran and the hadith.

After centuries of concise research, the authenticity of the *Kutub al-Sittah* (The Authentic Six Books) along with other hadith has been verified... There is a vast amount of information in regards to this in hadith books, those who are interested can refer to them.

If we can't understand the purpose and wisdom of a hadith, or what kind of an observation it's based on, we should at least observe the courtesy to remain silent and wait until we can understand.

Let us also remember that one day we will come face to face with the Rasul of Allah!

According to us...

Muhammad (saw) is a magnificent individual embellished with extraordinary qualities! Our honor is in respect to how much we can know and understand him!

Since the age of 18 I've been trying to understand and explain him, his teachings and the system in light of modern science, to the best of my capacity... Nevertheless, all that I've done in regards to understanding and teaching about him is 'nothing'...

Indeed, Muhammad (saw) is free from the absurd claims that reduce him to a courier!

Having clarified this, let's now move on to the supremacy of Risalah...

As I've previously explained, Gabriel's act of squeezing the Rasul of Allah (saw) enabled him to experience significant self-conquest (*fath*) in respect to some of the Names of Allah that became activated... Their activation, and thus a greater manifestation of these qualities, enabled his insight, foresight and introspection (i.e. the ability to become cognizant of the makeup, qualities, creational purpose and wisdom behind a particular unit of existence) to grow. This isn't something that can be attained suddenly… The act of squeezing increases a capacity in the brain, which takes time to incorporate. This is why after the first revelation it took three years for the next revelation to come; Gabriel did not visit Muhammad for three years.

In fact, during this time he even thought he was abandoned and thus much distressed.

But this time period was necessary. Time was needed for the first and powerful expansion, the capacity to perceive and evaluate the beings and data of one higher dimension to assimilate.

Though essentially he was already endowed with all of Allah's Names within his creational program, this experience activated and enhanced their effect and enabled him to READ the absolute truth, the universal system.

22

GABRIEL'S COURIER OR THE RASUL OF ALLAH

Normally, the general rule is to appoint a qualified person for a job, otherwise you'll not only do wrong by the job, but also by the person.

How can someone who was constantly in contact with Gabriel and other angels, who saw the jinn and interacted with them, who READ the system, who saw heaven and hell while living among us and explained the conditions of life in those dimensions, who observed the things that are experienced in the grave and gave news to those around him about the state of those who have passed on, who lead those who follow his path to innumerous extraordinary qualities, and whose phenomenal qualities we can't list, be reduced to a deliveryman/courier? Could he really have been unaware of the message he brought?

Let's put the conditions of today aside and think about all the countless saints and enlightened ones who came and passed on... Some observed the realities through discovery (*kashf*) and some through self-conquest (*fath*)... Which of them has claimed the hadith of the Rasul are fabrications and attempted to nullify them?

In fact, a significant majority of such eminent men have frequently had contact with the Rasul and heard these truths directly from him!

Had the hadith really been fabrication, surely the enlightened ones who are still able to contact and interact with the Rasul even today would have warned us.

The religion of Islam is protected by the manifestation of Allah's knowledge, will and power, it has lead hundreds and millions of people for centuries based on the hadith of the Rasul of Allah (saw), and each person has taken his share of this according to his own creational program.

The role of Muhammad (saw), Allah's Rasul, is far greater than the limited comprehension capacity of those who lack insight and spirituality!

The rank of the envoy is commensurate with the sender. Never does a president appoint his maintenance man as envoy!

Muhammad (saw) is Allah's Rasul and envoy! He's not the envoy of Gabriel, as some claim, or a god in space.

I wonder if those who think Muhammad (saw) was the envoy of Gabriel know with whom they are in agreement and whose effect they're under?

Whatever we may say in regard to the servant and envoy of Allah, it is inadequate! It is not possible for us to duly explain his sublimity!

So, let us not transgress our place any further and turn back to talking about his function and works and the magnificent system that he read!

23

READING THE SYSTEM

To live peacefully and benefit maximally from one's environment, one needs to know the conditions and lifestyle of the area in which one resides. Based on this, one can take the necessary precautions and protect oneself from any possible danger and attain favorable outcomes. So, at a most basic level, this is why it is necessary to decipher and comprehend the mechanics of the system, to READ it.

Even though Muhammad (saw) was endowed with the capacity to READ by his creation, the fact he couldn't yet activate this capability caused him much distress and drove him to retreat at Mount Hira.

The 'natural system of Allah' was generally conceived as:

You're born from random parents, you live your life to meet the necessities of the body (food, drink, sexuality, etc.) and then you leave everything behind and go.

On the other hand…

Does life continue after death?

Is there a god that controls and administers things from afar?

Do we have to give account for the things we did in this world?

If so, who is going to call us to account? A god in space, perhaps?

If such a god existed, where is he? How is he? How great is he?

Why did he create us in the first place? If he is free of need, why did he feel the need to create us?

Surely we couldn't be alone in the universe, the jinn also exist! How did we coexist with them? At which point could they affect us, if they can? And to what extent?

Such questions engaged the minds of the people back in those days, too...

The concept of god was clearly the pivotal point of all these questions.

What was it, where was it and how was it? Did it exist or not? Was it one or many?

Muhammad (saw) was probably also overwhelmed by such questions when he encountered the acclaimed amazing experience where Gabriel contacted him and told him to read the system using the divine power and knowledge already present within him.

For 23 years, Gabriel revealed the religion, that is, the system, to Muhammad.

Religion, in the sight of Allah, is Islam.

But what is Islam?

It is the natural disposition (fitrah)!

What is the natural disposition of the system?

We must first understand what religion is before we get to the natural disposition of the system.

Religion begins with understanding the reality denoted by the name Allah.[32]

It's important to understand the word religion and the system it references correctly and without contradiction. For this, a concise and comprehensive study of religion is necessary. This knowledge cannot be acquired from parents and Quran course instructors or those who've memorized the Quran but have no clue as to what it actually means. Otherwise, it will result in adverse situations.

---

[32] Refer to *Muhammad's Allah* for further information.

What matters is to know why you need to do what and for what purpose, to acknowledge and understand the life after death and thus shape your current life accordingly.

Life after death is the biggest reality for mankind. If we don't understand this, and prepare accordingly, we'll be doing the greatest wrong to ourselves.

Whatever you may possess in this world, whatever your rank or title may be, eventually you're going to be stripped away from all of it and placed among unknown forms of life with the power of your spirit and consciousness.

A wise person will use every opportunity to duly and adequately research and prepare for this arena. For nothing in existence can become nonexistent!

Despite the changes your body is subject to, there is a sense of 'I' inside, which is your consciousness, who is untouched and unaffected by it all. If this 'I' is unaffected by the changes of the body, then 'consciousness' is obviously not something physical. But it exists! Since nothing that exists can become nonexistent, then your individual consciousness (what was defined as the heart in old religious texts), your sense of self, is not going to be lost or become nonexistent once the function of the body becomes invalidated through death.

So then, what kind of a life is awaiting you…? Have you ever considered this?

This is what religion is concerned about and any individual who contemplates will inevitably have to consider these truths at some point in their life.

But let us first realize and comprehend the truth that there is no room for emotionality in nature!

The magnificent mechanism of Allah functions with all its might and without the interruption of emotions!

Thus, there is no room for excuses after death. Each will automatically live the consequences of their own deeds.

Hence, to blame others or claim you've heard this and that from this sheikh or that hodja will have no meaning or validity after death.

Either you can choose not to believe in life after death, in which case you're free to live as you like, provided you're willing to face any possible consequence...

Or, if you do believe in life after death, then you must leave aside what you've heard at school or home, or at this mosque or from that sheikh, and find out the truth for yourself.

This is something you need to do for yourself, because it's your life in the future!

Therefore, research is a must.

Why did the Nabi come, what does he advise and why?

Once you start searching for the answers to these questions you will begin to decipher the system...

Some who take things at a surface value claim religion is not based on a system and hence advocate the idea that religion comprises the commands of a god afar.

Intellect is the perception tool of consciousness. Something is either based on a logical system or it's absurd and meaningless. Every part of the perceivable existence is self-evidently ordered and systematized. This is why the Quran repeatedly questions, "Will you still not think? Will you still not use your intellect? We have revealed this Quran so that you will contemplate and understand!..." And so on...

The word 'reveal' (*inzal*) denotes a dimensional revelation, the process of a reality becoming revealed to one's consciousness. That is, it has to be understood in terms of dimensions not location. Otherwise, it would mean a physical revelation from space or from a particular location.

If the Quran wasn't a book of the system based on logical derivations, the above verses would not have been necessary.

In any case, a book talking about chaos and illogicality would have been irrelevant for conscious and intelligent beings!

The magnificent mechanism of Allah is such a perfect system that there is absolutely no room for any form of contradiction or disorder.

If some people perceive certain things as contradictory or disordered that is the result of a lack of insight and research concerning that particular topic.

24

THE BASMALAH

If the chapter al-Fatiha is understood well it can unlock the Quran for us.

For: "The secret of the Quran is in the Fatiha, the secret of the Fatiha is in the Basmalah, and the secret of the Basmalah is in the letter B!"

So, to enter the meaning of the Fatiha we must first discern the meaning of the Basmalah, but before we can do that we must first understand the secret of the letter B.

Those who have not understood the secret to which the letter B points think Allah is outside, somewhere far in space and call Him to account for the things they don't understand.

Those who've attained the secret of the letter B realize the infinity and illimitability of Allah and the 'nothingness' of the universe and themselves and enjoy the reality that Allah is the only timeless existence.

Just as the illusory sense of 'I' is the root cause of all suffering, the single cause for comfort and pleasure is the observation of one's nothingness within the concept of Allah.

That is, unity with Allah is through the secret of the letter B!

Why do we say the Basmalah before we recite the Fatiha? Because the Rasul of Allah (saw) says:

"Bismillahirrahmanirraheem is the key to all books."

Just as you can't unlock a door without its key, without understanding the letter B it's not possible to understand the meanings in the 'Book'! Only when we approach the topic with the consciousness of the letter B can we truly turn to the core of the matter and reach our target.

If we take heed of what the eminent saints and enlightened ones of the past have said, the reason why the Fatiha must be begun with the Basmalah is a warning about which state one must approach the topic.

"With the name of Allah, who is Rahman and Rahim, my being which subsists with the existence denoted by the name Allah, it is He who manifests this activity from me with His Grace...

The only absolute producer of my actions is Allah. I'm doing this action with the meanings denoted by the name Allah. It is His absolute essence (*dhat*), knowledge, power and wisdom that is behind my action..."

So, live with this consciousness and do not become veiled from the reality with beliefs that go against the truth.

Let's remember the warning that was made to Muhammad (saw), also a 'human' like us:

"And you threw not (the arrow) **when you** (illusory self; ego) **threw, but it was Allah who threw!"**[33]

And the verse:

"It is Allah who created you and all your doings!"[34]

---

[33] Quran 8:17
[34] Quran 37:96

This is why one who says the Basmalah before commencing any activity is implicitly saying:

"I begin this activity with the qualities and power, and as the wisdom of Allah, the Rahman, the Rahim. I realize and comprehend that He is the absolute doer and this activity is manifesting from me as His wish and command."

"You cannot will unless Allah wills (your will is Allah's will)**!"**[35]

That is to say, "I am nothing, my life belongs to Allah as the manifestation of His name '*Hayy*'. As the expression of His attribute of knowledge, consciousness and knowledge are disclosed through me. Due to His quality '*Mureed*', I am able to 'will' and with His power I am able to actualize my will!"

Another way to put it is:

Due to Allah being Rahman and Rahim, whatever manifests through me, as Earth's vicegerent (*khalifa*), is on His behalf. I'm not doing it as 'I' the illusory self, but as the manifestation of His Names, and therefore as Him."

One may wonder why the Basmalah is said silently while the Fatiha is recited out loud.

If the meaning of the Basmalah is well discerned, it will be clear that the Basmalah is something to be lived and experienced, not something to claim or state outwardly.

---

[35] Quran 76:30

25

THE FATIHA

'Hamd' belongs to Allah

The first verse says:

"Hamd (the evaluation of the corporeal worlds created with His Names, as He wills) **belongs to Allah!"**

I can almost hear you say, "How did this interpretation come about? We've never heard it like this! The meaning of this verse is generally known as: 'Praise belongs to Allah, the lord of the worlds, so let's praise only Allah, not other gods...'!"

Let me try to explain to the best of my ability...

Allah is *wahid-ul ahad*... That is, Allah is absolute oneness, no other existence besides Himself exists who can understand, administer, evaluate or praise Him!

Only Allah can know Allah, only Allah can evaluate Allah, only Allah can praise Allah!

As the Rasul of Allah (saw) says:

"I cannot duly praise You as You praise Yourself"

It's not possible for one who is at a lower state to praise one who is at a higher state. It's not possible for me to praise the Rasul, only Allah can praise the Rasul!

In order for someone to praise another, he must first encompass that person in every sense, then evaluate him, and then he can either praise him or criticize him.

If someone wants to praise or criticize me, for example, he must first encompass my knowledge.

I don't mean he needs to be a graduate from this or that institution or have such and such title. I mean he has to be at a level of consciousness that encompasses the capacity of knowledge that manifests from me.

Only after this can he comprehensively and adequately evaluate my thoughts and derivations, determine whether they are correct or incorrect, praise or criticize them!

To criticize an idea that's beyond your comprehension, without such a capacity, can be nothing other than rumor and idle chatter.

Therefore, it is neither possible for me to evaluate and appraise someone higher than me or for any form of creation to praise and evaluate Allah!

Thus, the verse confirms, "*Hamd* belongs only to Allah! The act of *hamd*, i.e. the evaluation of the corporeal worlds, pertains only to Allah!"

Let us contemplate with some insight...

Think of the place of a single human on earth!

Now think of his place in the sight of the Sun, which is 1 million times bigger than the Earth!

Then think of his place in the galaxy, containing billions of stars like the Sun!

And then his place in the universe comprises billions of galaxies!

Now think of Allah, the creator of all of this, plus the infinite universes that we can't perceive and of which we have no idea!

Can you comprehend it?

How much of the infinite universe embellished with the infinite qualities of the infinite *wahid-ul ahad* can we appraise and evaluate, let alone evaluate and praise Allah!

There is a story that Rumi narrates:

One day while Moses is on his way somewhere he hears someone talking near a tree. He curiously goes towards the tree only to see a shepherd sitting under the tree talking to himself. He wonders what he's saying so he quietly listens. The shepherd says: "O my beautiful Allah, how I wish You were by my side right now, I would have loved You and hugged You, I would have fed You fresh milk, I would have laid You down on my lap and made You rest in the shade and I would have removed Your lice and nits…"

Obviously at this point Moses loses his patience and exclaims: "Be silent, o foolish one! How dare you think you can lay Allah down, feed Him milk, and even remove nits and lice from Him when He is the Rabb of the worlds and the possessor of absolute might and sublimity! Do you not know Allah is free from such things!?"

The poor shepherd is taken aback and frightened, "I'm so sorry, please forgive me, I didn't know… It's just that I love him so! I'm just a poor shepherd; my only wealth is my Allah! I sit with Him, walk with Him, eat with Him and sleep with Him! My only friend and beloved is Him! I was told He is always with me, so I took Him as my friend, that's why I spoke like this… But I will never say such things again! So you say He's far greater and bigger than all of this, huh!? Oh my… Now what will I do…?"

Moses taught him how to supplicate and pray and went on his way…

As he was walking away thinking about the state of the shepherd he heard him calling out, "Moses! Moses!" When he turned around he saw the shepherd walking on water towards him…. At this point it is revealed to Moses: "O Moses, you separated My friend from Me who had turned to Me with his whole being, who had no other thought other than Me, you built great walls between us! Immediately destroy the walls you built and unite Me with My friend again!"

Moses learnt his lesson and realized that, just as Allah manifests Himself with all His might and awe to some, to some He manifests as sincerity and purity…

So he turned to the shepherd and says, "Forget about what I told you, keep doing what you've been doing, turn to Him and talk to Him as you always did! He's closer to you than you are to yourself!"

Either we're going to praise Him like the poor shepherd or be realistic and say, "*Hamd* belongs to Allah, we're impotent in this area!" and realize our 'nothingness' and know our place. Allah does not like the transgressors.

In short, *hamd* is an act that belongs to Allah. And He is free from a partner.

The Quran warns us with the first verses of the Fatiha:

"Be sound in your judgment and do not think of Him as a simple heavenly god, praising and exalting Him to win His favor. You're impotent from duly appraising Him. Only Allah can evaluate and do *hamd* to Allah. What befits you is to realize your inadequacy in this area and know your place!"

We've also been warned by Abu Bakr (ra), whose degree in the sight of the Rasul is well known:

"To comprehend Allah is to comprehend that He is incomprehensible!"

The ultimate truth Islam underlines is that the only absolute existence is the infinite limitless Oneness, and nothing exists besides It!

Everything that we perceive and that is perceived by all forms of creation is assumed compositions of the meanings of His Names.

This being the case, one is left with nothing else to say other than, "*Hamd* belongs to Allah," which, as the qualified would know, is quite a noble state!

It is the state of observing Allah with Him from your state of nothingness!

Yes, *hamd* belongs to Allah, it is His right, only He can do *hamd*, it is under Allah's administration, only He can evaluate, because only Allah exists, there is nothing other than Him in existence… He who knows this knows this, he who doesn't, knows nothing!

Moving on to the next phrase:

"**The Rabb** (the absolute source of the infinite meanings of the Names) **of the worlds** (the universe created within the brain of every individual)**"**

The word Rabb essentially means 'tame', here it's been used as 'the one who tames' and the act of taming is known as '*Rububiyyah*'…

To tame is to guide something level by level to its point of perfection…

Rabb is one who prepares, develops and matures all forms of creation to ensure they actualize their creational purpose. In short, it is the one who manifests the forms at their current state.

The properties of 'Rabb' are the Names of Allah. That is, *Rububiyyah* is comprised of the Names of Allah.

Everything we can or can't perceive is created and continues its existence with the Names of Allah – which is the very taming of the Rabb.

This is established with the verse:

"There is no animate being that He does not hold (program with the Name *Fatir*) **by its forehead** (brain) (i.e. subjugate to His command)."[36]

Thus, every perceivable and unperceivable thing is forever subject to His knowledge and administration, and continues its existence and acts with His power.

As for 'the worlds'…

Every unit (note that I'm saying 'unit' not human, angel, jinn or animal, etc.) perceives its own dimension; this is its 'world'! In this light, it's correct to say every unit is itself a world! For everything that is perceived is no other than a collection of images in the mind of that unit!

The things we see are images formed in our brain. When we claim to see something we are actually saying:

Electromagnetic signals coming into my brain from outside are processed according to my already existing database to form this image! The things I'm perceiving are taking these forms and images according to my mind!

But is this is the absolute truth?

Indeed, all things we perceive are various compositions of the Names of Allah, reflecting to our consciousness…

To summarize the meaning of the phrase, "*Hamd* belongs to the Rabb of the worlds":

To comprehend and evaluate Allah, who creates all units as He wills and who guides them to their point of perfection in a way most suitable to their creational purpose, is not something the units can do, *Hamd* belongs only to Allah, the Rabb of all things!

---

[36] Quran 11:56

26

HELL IS GRACE

The Rahman is the possessor of grace, who forms all things from Himself with Himself.

The forms of grace can be divided into two: absolute grace and attribute-based grace. It can further be categorized as general grace and specific grace.

Absolute grace refers to the fact that the existence of all beings depends on the Absolute Essence of Allah, thus it is said the grace of Allah encompasses all things.

Attribute-based grace refers to the notion that all meanings that become manifest on all beings depend on the Names of Allah in their original state (before their compositional states).

General grace is the most comprehensive grace, it is with this grace that all sufferings in the afterlife will eventually end one day, even if they've been confined to hell eternally. The grace of the Rahman covers even those in hell!

Even though the Quran says some will remain in hell forever, it does not say they will forever be subject to suffering. This is the result of general grace.

A common question is, "If Allah has so much grace, why does he cast people to hell in the first place?"

Why hell?

Hell is one of the most misunderstood concepts in religion.

Why has hell been created?

Are there residents in hell?

What are the creatures of hell?

Why do people go to hell?

Why do people burn in hell?

Are there different types of burning?

What is hellfire like?

How can one continue to live in fire?

Unfortunately, illogical and absurd answers to such questions have forever pushed people away from understanding...

The word hell has a general meaning and a specific meaning.

In general, it means the state and environment in which people are subject to suffering.

In this sense we can talk about hell on earth, hell in the grave and hell at the place of gathering (mahshar)... The prison, hospital or other environments to which you are confined, for example, may be like hell for you; these are all relative forms of hell. Even the hell that is experienced in the realm of the grave is a relative form of hell.

There is also an absolute hell, which according to my observations, is the Sun. Not in the format that we perceive it right now, but as its radial twin that also currently exists. Those who die and pass on to Earth's radial twin can see this.

Eventually the Sun is going to be 400 times bigger than its current size, engulfing Mercury, Venus, the Earth and the Moon, and reaching the orbit of Mars. It's going to be 400 million times bigger than the Earth!

That's when all the spirits that are subject to Earth's magnetic field, that is, humans with holographic bodies, are going to want to escape from Earth, as Earth loses its magnetic pull.

Those who've practiced the recommended practices, such as prayer and dhikr –all of which have been advised to strengthen one's spiritual energy rather than as an offering to a god – will be able to escape the Earth and the Sun's flames of radiation… This has been symbolized as the bridge of '*sirat*'!

The flames of hell have been called '*samum*' in the Quran, which means toxic destructive radiation.

The Sun's radiation, which destroys matter and burns and deforms the radial bodies of people, comprises the gigantic flames of hell, which even today reach 800,000 km in height! Imagine their size when the Sun is 400 times bigger!

There are two types of suffering in hell.

The first is physical; the second is spiritual and thought-based.

Physical burning is when the photons of the highly heated radiation of hell deforms and destroys the radial makeup… The second is the burning that will occur when the false information and conditioning in one's mind is invalidated and destroyed.

This is primarily due to one's ego, the sense of self, possessiveness, ambition, thinking you are the body and thus living in pursuit of bodily pleasures.

Think about the sense of burning you feel when you lose something you own. Whereas if you can just say "Allah gave it, Allah took it" your suffering is going to end immediately, perhaps you're not going to suffer at all.

Essentially what constitutes the sense of suffering (or burning) in hell is the environmental conditionings, the value judgments resulting from them and the emotions that spawn from them.

Whenever you find yourself saying, "This *must* be like this" or "it *has* to be like that" behold, you're going to suffer, it's inevitable!

For, like it or not, at some point it's going to change or turn into something else, and this is going to cause you to suffer!

The great majority of the people start suffering while still living on Earth. Some start suffering upon death, after departing their biological bodies, as this is the biggest loss of what they thought they owned!

So, why is suffering a grace?

Why do people of paradise burn in hell first?

Because one can only go to paradise if one is completely free from their conditionings and incorrect value judgments, and this only happens via burning.

Grace causes one to burn, to suffer and become cleansed! Burning rids one of unrealistic thoughts, emotions and conditionings!

People suffer when they encounter ideas or situations that go against their conditioned beliefs. If the person can get over their fear of 'what others might think or say' and proceed towards their true purpose, in alignment with their beliefs they will be saved from most of their suffering…

Adopting and practicing the truths of Sufism enables one to recognize their essential reality and saves them from burning while still on Earth. If there was no hell and we weren't subject to the cleansing process through burning, we could never reach and experience the state of paradise.

Thus, burning is actually an amazing mechanism of mercy and grace, similar to amputation done to remove a diseased organ.

As for the creatures of hell…

There are conscious beings specific to each level and dimension of life. Just as there are conscious life forms on every planet, every layer of existence in the universe also has forms of life specific to them, all of which have been referenced as 'angels' in religious terminology.

Because our brains have been programmed to evaluate only the data received through the five senses, we are oblivious to all the life forms that fall outside this perception range. Yet, besides all the life forms on other planets, we're not even aware of the jinn who constantly try to manipulate and affect our brains!

The Quran refers to the conscious creatures that live in the Sun as *'zabani'*. They are also a type of angel. Due to their luminous knowledge (*nur*)-based makeup and the fact they are formed within that environment, they live under what may seem extreme conditions to us, without being adversely affected, like water is the natural living environment for fish.

They have extremely large bodies and the ability to move very quickly compared to other beings. Just like fish dwell in water, swallow water and breathe water, the *zabani* dwell in fire, they eat and breathe fire. They play with the humans and jinn that go there as though playing with a ball, picking on and bullying them for not listening to those who warned them about hell…

Just like we think we have the liberty to treat animals however we like, caging them, taming them, punishing them to teach them certain skills and domesticate them, the *zabani* do the same to those in their living environment, oblivious to whether this causes them suffering!

The word *zabani* means 'to degrade, humiliate, insult, etc.' They are domineering and commanding beings of such enforcing power that anyone that is subject to their harassment is bound to be ridiculed, insulted, degraded and caused to suffer. Similar to some people who are possessed by the jinn and end up on the streets miserable and distraught, or the circus animals who are put through so much torture or the animals used in laboratories for experimental purposes!

No doubt, the best thing to do is to avoid such places!

I'm assuming I've sufficiently explained why hell is grace and, contrary to common thought, people aren't sent to hell so they suffer but as the natural consequence of their actions that results from their incorrect thoughts and emotions, that is, suffering is the resulting effect of such false conditionings.

As a side note, if only those who are moralized with the morals of Allah can enter paradise, what then are the morals of Allah? Something to think about...

Now on to specific grace…

Specific grace is a distinct form of grace, specified for those whom He has chosen for Himself…

"Allah chooses for Himself whom He wills"[37]

"He is not questioned (called to account) for what He does!"[38]

First He rids the servant whom He chooses for Himself from 'hidden duality', the ego-identity and the concept of an external god, then he moralizes him with His own morals, then He rewards him with 'unveiling' (*kashf*) and self-conquest (*fath*), enabling him to experience the life of paradise! Beyond this is only known to those who experience it!

There is also another meaning denoted by the name 'Rahim'.

We said the grace denoted by Rahman is related to cleansing, which inevitably causes some form of pain and suffering. Though the amputation of an organ is seemingly an intense form of suffering, the fact it's done with the purpose of saving one's life causes us to thank the surgeon rather than be upset with him. This kind of grace, which initially causes pain and suffering, but is essentially for a beneficial outcome, is Rahman-based grace.

The grace of the Rahim, on the other hand, is not for the purpose of cleansing or teaching, but purely to give pleasure via beauteous experiences. This is the kind of grace that will be experienced in the life of paradise.

However, let us be mindful that the Names of Allah are constantly in effect. Hence, to think the meaning of the name Rahim is currently ineffective and will only be in effect in paradise is a complete misconception. The name Rahim is in effect at every instance, whether we realize this or not.

There are many people who have and who currently are experiencing the manifestation of this Name on Earth, while others only experience it in paradise, perhaps without even knowing how and why it is formed.

---

[37] Quran 42:13
[38] Quran 21:23

Besides the people of unveiling and self-conquest, the people of certainty, the people of authenticity and the people of gnosis of Allah are still consciously experiencing and observing the manifestation of the name Rahim in light of the letter B.

The meaning of the expression, 'La hawla wala kuwwata illa B'illah' is also from the Rahim.

Thus, it is utterly incorrect to think the name Rahim will only be in effect in paradise, in the life after death, especially when infinite amounts of angels are constantly subject to the effect of this Name!

27

WHAT IS 'THE DAY OF RELIGION'?

Maleek (or maalik) **yawmiddeen...**

The Maalik or Maleek of the day of religion.

Some take this word as Maalik and some as Maleek:

The Maleek (the Sovereign One, who manifests His Names as He wishes and governs them in the world of acts as He pleases. The One who has providence over all things) or the Maalik (the Absolute Owner) of the eternal period governed by the decrees of religion (sunnatullah).

Essentially, Allah is both Maleek and Maalik, but since the phrase 'the day of religion' is used, we have to consider the grammatical rules according to the context in which it has been used.

Religion can be understood as 'reaching the results of one's deeds' and as 'absolute submission,' but religion cannot be interpreted as Doomsday!

Due to not realizing that the results and consequences of our deeds are met at 'every instance,' people have conceived it as the 'last day' as though everyone is going to meet the consequences of their deeds on that last day!

Let us remember the first verse of chapter al-Maun:

"Did you see the one who denies his religion (the sunnatullah)**?"**[39]

That is, did you see the one who denies the system and order of Allah?

Since one day during the period of *mahshar* is going to be equivalent to 50,000 Earth years and thus the experience of *mahshar* and the crossing of the Bridge of *Sirat* is going to take thousands and thousands of years, it is unrealistic to think all of this is going to transpire in one day, a single day of which Allah is the Maalik or Maleek.

My observation is, in the sight of Allah, there is one instance among other instances that the word 'day' refers to. This day, comprising a single instance in the sight of Allah, is in our sight, pre- and post-eternal, and everything is in absolute submission to Him. That is, the manifestations of His Maalik and Maleek qualities are eternal!

You may wonder, many commit great crimes and get away with it in this world, doesn't this prove that the day of facing consequences is in fact a day in the afterlife?

This very question is an indication of the concept of an external god and thus lack of discernment regarding Allah.

Everyone is at every instance face to face with the consequences of their previous action, for "Allah is sari'ul hisab" (swift at reckoning).

But, due to our inadequacy to duly evaluate the conditions the person is subject to after his action, we think he got away with it in the world and that he'll be punished in the afterlife.

---

[39] Quran 107:01

But Allah also uses divine deception (*makr*)!

Many are subject to the results of their deeds through divine deception!

Wealth, children, rank and status, fame and so on are all vehicles of trial and those who aren't awake are prone to becoming carried away and deceived by such provocations, as the Quran explicitly states.

Many are given wealth only to invest it in property and worldly possessions, rather than spending it in the way of Allah! Those who see their seeming wealth may think they've been blessed whereas in reality they've been given that wealth as divine deception due to a wrong done.

So, without even realizing, they will spend their days spending wealth in pursuit of worldly pleasures falling far from union with Allah and losing many opportunities that they'll never have the chance to regain in the future.

Even though the Rasul of Allah (saw) was the proprietor of a successful trading business, he spent everything he owned in the way of Allah, leaving nothing behind when he passed away.

Likewise, Hadhrat Abu Bakr spent all his wealth in the way of Allah and greeted death in poverty.

Wealth given as divine deception can never be spent in the way of Allah!

Yet many see people living in great wealth and worldly pleasures and think they aren't subject to the consequences of their actions.

The truth is their very wealth is the consequence of their misdeeds given to them as divine deception veiling them from Allah more and more every day.

Nothing is a greater punishment than being veiled from Allah.

If we realize this, we will understand that every moment of our lives is the day of religion!

At every moment we are in absolute submission to Allah, whether it be through divine blessing or deception, at every instance of our lives we are subject to the consequences of our prior actions.

Thus, the 'Maalik of the Day of Religion' is only Him, and only to Him does the entire existence submit, and it is He who creates the results of every action that's done.

As such, all meanings pertaining to Allah must be understood as applicable at all times rather than a particular point in time.

28

WHAT IS SERVITUDE?

"You alone we serve, and from You alone we seek help"[40]

This verse is commonly construed as:

"We only worship You, not others, and only seek help from You, not others," which obviously implies the concept of 'others'.

But, if we look at it from the point of 'unity of existence' which is what we've been trying to explain since the beginning of this book, then the meaning can be understood as:

Since You are the Rabb of the worlds, and thus also my Rabb, and the Maalik and Maleek of the Day of Religion, and since we all exist with Your Names, it follows that everything at every instance is in servitude to You, whether we realize it or not...

We fulfill our absolute servitude to You by manifesting your Names, each of which is based on a different wisdom.

And each of us (man, jinn, angels) awaits Your help at every instance for the continuation of our servitude. If You stop expressing and manifesting the meanings of Your Names that comprise our being we will become nonexistent!

---

[40] Quran 1:5

We seek Your help for the continuation of our existence and servitude.

"I have created the jinn and men only so that they may serve Me (by means of manifesting the qualities of My Names).**"**[41]

Therefore, it is not possible for creation not to be in servitude!

Many have interpreted this verse as though it is only in reference to salat, whereas if we notice, the verse is in the first chapter, which explains the system and order of Allah, and its meaning is valid and effective at all times, pre- and post-eternally!

Whether it be during salat or outside salat, whenever it is recited it references and encompasses the whole of creation and all of its states.

"There is nothing that does not exalt (*tasbih*) **Him with hamd** (evaluation of the corporeal worlds created with His Names, as He wills)!**"**[42]

This verse clearly and openly explicates this truth leaving no room for interpretation.

After the starting verses, which according to my understanding elucidate the truth that the One denoted by the name Allah is the Rabb of the worlds, this verse emphasizes the fact that everything in existence is in servitude to Him and they are forever in need of Him to continue their servitude!

The verse, **"I have created the jinn and men only so that they may serve Me** (by means of manifesting the qualities of My Names)**"**[43] also points to the same reality.

––––––––––––––––––––

[41] Quran 51:56
[42] Quran 17:44
[43] Quran 51:56

If one is created to fulfill servitude, is it at all possible for them not to?

Let us remember the Fatir, and how Allah defines Himself as the Fatir of the heavens and the earth… That is, He forms, creates and equips everything according to whichever meaning He wishes to manifest through them.

And of course the verse:

"Your Rabb has ordered you to serve only Him."[44]

But how are we to understand and evaluate this?

Since Allah is the Rabb of the worlds, He has willed to observe the infinite meanings of His Names and has thus manifested them as compositions to comprise creation.

And since all creation is composed of these meanings, they don't have another existence besides this. Therefore, by their very act of manifesting these meanings, they fulfill their absolute servitude.

With a little insight, it is evident to see all the verses above are actually pointing to this truth.

To construe these verses, which encompass all of the meanings pertaining to the whole of creation, in an exceedingly limited way, as if the person performing salat is confessing his servitude to his Rabb and seeking His help, goes against the universality of the Quran.

But do they not have a point? Doesn't this verse imply a confession of servitude and a seeking of help? Have those who've construed it this way completely misunderstood it?

It is not incorrect, only inadequate and shallow, thus a very limited understanding; this is only a very small aspect of the actual matter.

---

[44] Quran 17:23

If "**You alone we serve, and from You alone we seek help**" is understood as "at every instance and with every breath" then there is no problem.

One may wonder, if everything is fulfilling its servitude by carrying out its creational purpose, then what's the point of prayer and worship? Why should we pray? Do we pray because we deify Allah? Can we earn the privilege of going to paradise if we engage in worship? Do people go to hell because they don't pray and worship?

There are two forms of servitude. The first is absolute servitude, which is what I've explained above. In this sense, all things are created for absolute servitude and they fulfill this at every instance, as the verse clearly defines:

"**I have created the jinn and men only so that they may serve Me** (by means of manifesting the qualities of My Names)."[45]

The second is relative servitude; it is the individual's recognition of Allah as their Rabb and the purpose of their existence to serve Him and the seeking of His continual help to fulfill this. Relative servitude is thus individual servitude.

Now we come to an interesting point... The Rasul of Allah (saw) says, "Salat is the ascension of the believer" and "Salat cannot be without the Fatiha."

"**So, woe to those who pray** (out of custom), **who are heedless** (cocooned) **of** (the experience of the meaning of) **their salat** (which is an ascension [*miraj*] to their innermost essential reality; their Rabb)"[46]

---

45 Quran 51:56
46 Quran 107:4-5

That is, those who perform salat unconsciously will inevitably be miserable!

The purpose of salat is ascension.

If this purpose isn't reached, one is veiled from Allah, and thus in great loss.

The experience of ascension is based on the discernment of the words in the Fatiha. So, one should wonder... Which meaning is in the Fatiha that isn't in all the other chapters in the Quran, that when it's not recognized and discerned, salat is rendered invalid? What is this meaning that, when experienced, enables one to live ascension?

The topics of basmalah, hamd and guidance are covered in other chapters of the Quran, so then the crux of this chapter is the verse "Malik-Maleek-i yawmiddeen; iyyaka nabudu wa iyyaka nastain" the verse in which the secret of fanafillah (annihilation of the self in Allah) is contained.

The expression, "iyyaka nabudu" is the expression of fanafillah.

Also, let's remember Rasulullah's (saw) words:

"The five (daily) salat (prayers) and the Friday (prayer) to the Friday (prayer) expiate whatever (minor sins) may be committed in between, so long as major sins are avoided."

So then, which meaning is contained in these verses that, when recognized and understood, expiates the mistakes done since the previous salat and opens the way to ascension?

Now, read the verse again! This is a very significant secret here!

As for deifying Allah...

Deification is something that has been done subconsciously for centuries in various forms, such as begging, exalting, offerings to idols, etc... This has nothing to do with the essence of prayer and worship, which is what servitude is all about.

Ibn Abbas (ra) says the word 'serve' (liya'budoon) in the verse **"I have created the jinn and men only so that they may serve Me..."** should be understood as 'liya'rifoon,' which refers to gnosis. In this light, if the expression 'iyyaka nabudu' in the Fatiha is also in reference to gnosis, then the above verse can be construed as the following:

"With the consciousness that Allah, the Rabb of the worlds, is our Rabb, we acknowledge that we are at every instance observing His administration upon existence, and for the continuation of this conscious servitude, we seek His help."

But do we not engage in prayer and worship so we can go to paradise?

Yet another misconception!

Nobody can go to paradise because of their worship!

The Rasul of Allah (saw) in a well-known hadith says:

"Nobody can go to paradise because of their deeds."

When asked, "Even you O Rasul of Allah (saw)?" He said, "Yes, even me! However, my Rabb has endowed His grace upon me (thus, I shall go to paradise not because of my deeds, but because of the grace of my Rabb)..."

This has to do with fate![47]

In short, no prayer or worship should be done to go to paradise, nowhere does it state those who worship will go to paradise; going to paradise has nothing to do with the prayer and worship the person does.

However, it is not incorrect to say Allah has eased the practice of worship to those who are destined to go to paradise.

Worship is to strengthen and increase one's awareness! Those who engage in prayer and worship can raise their level of consciousness... But the primary factor behind one who can engage in these practices is that Allah has destined paradise for that person.

---

[47] The topic of fate has been covered extensively in *The Mystery of Man* and *Akil ve Iman (Turkish)*

If he's not destined to go, no matter how much he prays, no matter how conscious and strong he becomes, he still cannot go!

In short, going to paradise has nothing to do with worship and everything to do with the nur of faith endowed by Allah!

Why does being freed from hell depend on faith?

There are some cases of paralysis that are totally psychological. Even though there is no pathological problem in the body, the person delusively believes he's paralyzed and that he will never be able to walk again and thus lives hell in his wheelchair. Hypochondriacs cannot duly evaluate their intellects or use their skills because of the grip of paranoia upon them and thus they live in misery!

Paranoia, to assume something into existence when it doesn't or assume it doesn't exist when it does – which turns one's world into hell – cannot be overcome by mind power or intellect. The only force that can overcome this is 'faith'!

Paranoia can easily rule over the mind and mechanism of thought, yet it is always defeated by faith, which directly affects one's actions.

Thus, religion has been offered to the intelligent, that they may understand it, yet faith is advised, that they may experience it.

Whether it be hell on earth or in the life after death, it is always the result of paranoia and only the force of faith can end it for good.

When the person who believes he is paralyzed encounters one in whom he can believe, he will be able to walk again; when the hypochondriac meets one in whom he can believe, his misery will end.

As such, belief in Allah enables one to believe he can overcome any adversity with the qualities of Allah inherent within his essence. With this faith and conviction, he can find the strength with which he can be freed from the state of hell, even if it's an iota's weight of faith! But if he doesn't have any faith, if he limits himself only to what he knows about himself, i.e. if he doesn't know Allah and does not believe in Allah, he will never be able to discover the forces and qualities pertaining to Allah within his essence, and thus he will forever be confined to hell. And nobody can help him if he doesn't believe, just like nobody can make the man who believes he is paralyzed walk again!

In other words, those who are to be confined to hell forever are those who have not been able to free themselves from suspicion and paranoia and who haven't really believed.

The word servitude actually means submission. It is to fulfill a task in a perfect manner without asking any questions or having any doubts. Essentially, all of creation does this naturally and automatically by default. Everything is in a state of servitude and submission.

However, to do this duly is to be conscious of it, to feel Him within you, and to experience awe as a result...

Otherwise, worship and servitude will only be done formally and superficially, on a superficial level, which will never generate the joy and pleasure that comes about when it's done consciously.

29

WHAT IS GUIDANCE AND HOW IS IT FORMED?

"Guide us to the straight path (sirat al-mustaqeem)."

The path that is best for us…

Guidance is the enabling of the realization that leads to one's innermost essential reality. It is to gracefully lead one to that which is best for them from within their own essence.

The most general definition of guidance is the easing of the path that leads each form of creation to that which is best for it via the name Latif…

Indeed, everyone has been determined a purpose to which they will reach though guidance, for that is what has been made easy for them.

Take myself, for example… I write these books as this is what has been determined for me, perhaps many who read it are not even going to duly evaluate and benefit from them… Perhaps many are going to read and say, "Nice books, interesting points…" Yet continue to live in their accustomed ways rather than applying these truths to their lives.

And perhaps some are going to claim, "This is nothing but nonsense and absurdity!" and toss it aside…

Yet maybe some are going to read it and, with the guidance endowed to them, recognize this as another aspect of the truth and begin evaluating the Quran from this perspective, understanding the universal system the Quran explains, the place and nature of man within this system and how man should prepare for his life in the future...

But there are some people who have come from closed societies, limited to the conservative conditionings of their environment and thus confined to a cocooned existence at an early age. So much so that even the practices they engage in later on in their lives cannot free them from their cocoons, forcing them to see everything from a very narrow perspective.

They travel abroad, see the world, study internationally and yet can't break free from the seemingly genuine, yet extremely limited, identity imposed upon them by their home environment.

They still think the Quran was miraculously sent from the sky to Muhammad (saw) in Mecca in order to teach good morals – first to the Arabs then to the rest of the world – commanding that none should be deified and worshipped other than Allah, and comprising lists of good and bad, right and wrong, etc.

According to them, the Quran is devoid of a system; it is absurd to look for clues of scientific truths in the Quran; neither medicine nor astronomy, physics, chemistry, etc., can be learnt from the Quran! The Quran is only a book that explains why and how the god in space has to be deified and worshipped and which rules the people need to abide by...

If Allah does not endow guidance to such a person, it is near impossible for him to break free from the cocoon formed during his early years.

To think in light of modern findings, freely and objectively, and especially to be open and cocoon-free in terms of the future, is infinite freedom.

Put my books aside, the number of people who actually 'read' the Quran is no more than a few! Beyond those who read the Quran 'to be rewarded with paradise' or to 'offer comfort to the dead,' how many actually read the Quran?

How many do you think read the Quran to contemplate on and discern the magnificent system, the qualities and makeup of those who are subject to that system, and the infinite manifestations of Allah's knowledge and power it explains; how many recognize this and experience awe before it?

The lecturers, preachers and sermonizers who have plenty to say when it comes to talking, yet not enough intellectual evidence when it comes to carrying their argument through, can do nothing more than address another's cocoon from their own cocoons:

"Beware! Do not heed books that invite you to think, to look with a wider perspective, to break out of your cocoon and fly! Ignore the modern blessings of Allah and keep thinking like those from a thousand years ago – that the Earth is the center of the universe and everything revolves around it! The Quran isn't a book of knowledge! It is not right to interpret it in the light of science! Let go of these new ideas lest you commit blasphemy and become misguided!"

Why is this so?

The primary reason is because the guidance that has come to them ordains it to be so! The divine will has decreed it so!

The seeming reason, however, is that even though their bodies have travelled the world, their intellects have not gone beyond the narrow mindset with which they've been conditioned by their environments, i.e. their cocoons!

In religious terms, one can say such people have not been 'given the ease' of considering views outside their cocoon worlds.

Those who haven't been brought up with freedom of thought, who've been confined to their conditioned beliefs, cannot see the truth even when it is in plain sight.

Thus, we cannot blame them; in fact, we must be tolerant towards them and understand that they are also upon guidance by Allah's determining.

Indeed, that which is eased for a person has much to do with the path that the 'Guider' has determined for him!

Hadhrat Ali (ra) narrates:

One time we were at a funeral, the Rasul of Allah (saw) came and sat by our side. We gathered around him. He was holding a staff. He put his head down and in a reflective way he started drawing lines in the dirt with the staff, then said, "Every single one of you without exception has been determined his place in either paradise or hell! It has been definitely determined whether you are of the fortunate or the unfortunate ones!" One of us asked, "O Rasul of Allah (saw), shall we then abandon our deeds and go by whatever has been written?" The Rasul of Allah (saw) answered, "The fortunate ones will engage in the deeds of the fortunate ones... The unfortunate ones will commit the deeds of the unfortunate ones... So, keep up your deeds, for it has already been eased for you! If you are of the fortunate ones, then your deeds will be eased for you, if you are of the unfortunate ones, then the deeds of the unfortunate will be eased for you!"

Another narration in relation to this one is by Omar's (ra) son, Abdullah:

Omar (ra) asks, "O Rasul of Allah (saw), are the things we are currently doing formed now or had they already been formed and completed?"

The Rasul (saw) answered, "O Son of Hattab, everything has been predetermined! Everyone is prepared for what has already been determined for him: the fortunate ones will work for their fortune and the unfortunate ones will work for their misfortune!"

And a final hadith about this topic before I move on to how the process of easing works...

Suraka bin Jush'm asks the Rasul (saw), "O Rasul of Allah! Are deeds formed due to what has been written by the Pen that writes the fates, in which case everything has already been written and the ink has already dried, or do they form in the future, without being predetermined?" The Rasul (saw) answered, "Your deeds have been predetermined by fate and written by the Pen, the ink of which has already dried! Whatever you have been created for is what will be eased for you!"

So, how is this process of easing and guidance carried out?

I had explained above that guidance was administered by the name Latif.

Let me try and explain what this means, after I share the following words by the Rasul (saw):

"Indeed, Allah the Sublime created everything in darkness, then shed His light (*nur*) upon them; those who took a share of this light are rightly guided, while those who didn't are misguided. Then the ink of the Pen dried."

Let's also remember the verses:

"Allah guides (enables the observation of His innermost essential reality) **to whom He wills."**[48]

"And He leads to the reality by the (Names comprising the essence of the) **stars** (the people of the reality, the hadith: 'My Companions are like the stars; whoever among them you follow, you will reach the truth')**...!"**[49]

"And the stars are subjected by and in service to His command (the stars are also a manifestation of the meanings of the Names comprising their essence)**..."**[50]

---

[48] Quran 22:16
[49] Quran 16:16
[50] Quran 16:12

"He governs the earth (the brain) **from the heaven** (through the cosmic electromagnetic energy emanating from the qualities of the Names in the form of celestial constellations [star signs] that affect the second brain in the gut and thus one's consciousness, or from an internal perspective, through the Names that become manifest in one's brain based on the holographic reality)...**"**[51]

"It is Allah who created the seven heavens, and of the earth, the like of them. His command continually (without interruption) **manifests between them** (astrological [angelic] influences that are also manifestations of Allah's Names and their effect on creation).**"**[52]

"Who created you (manifested you)**, formed you** (with a brain, an individual consciousness and a spirit) **and balanced you** (the work process of your brain, consciousness and spirit)**! Whatever form** (manifestation of Names) **He willed for you, He configured your composition accordingly."**[53]

Imam Ghazali writes in his *Ihya-u Ulumuddeen* that ibn Abbas (ra) one of the scholars among the disciples says:

"If I were to interpret the meaning of the verse **'It is Allah who created the seven heavens, and of the earth, the like of them. His command continually** (without interruption) **manifests between them'** surely you would call me an unbeliever and stone me to death!"

"He governs the earth (the brain) **from the heaven..."**

---

[51] Quran 32:05
[52] Quran 65:12
[53] Quran 82:7-8

"And the stars are subjected by and in service (with the rays they permeate) **to His command** (the stars are also a manifestation of the meanings of the Names comprising their essence)**..."**[54]

So, what is their duty?

Surely they haven't been created to adorn the skies with their pretty lights?

Let's be realistic and see things objectively for what they really are rather than how we'd like to see them…

Since Allah is the infinite existence, there is no other existence besides Him. Everything we see and label is His conscious forms, existent and subsistent with the meanings of His Names.

Their only difference is the degree of manifestation of the various Names in their composition. Thus, it is always Allah who governs through every unit of existence and interacts with other units, guides, shapes and aids towards their purpose of existence.

There is no other Creator, Rabb, Guider, Mahdi, Muyhi, Mumit besides Him! But, because we don't really comprehend this, we interpret things in ways that indicate denial.

Either we exalt Him beyond our imagination, beyond the heavens, beyond or further away from anything we can ever fathom! Or, we reduce Him to everything we can see; claiming every 'thing' is Him and thus limiting His infinite existence to His manifestations, even claiming our individuality to be Him!

Or else, we try to prove 'everything' exists, that you and I and him and her and every other being also exist alongside with Allah, yet again applying a limitation to Him! And then we talk at random about the things He makes us do!

Just as an author can't be defined by the characters he creates in his works, Allah can't be defined by or limited to His creations. Indeed, the power and meaning that is manifest under the label of

---

[54] Quran 16:12

existence belongs to Him alone… All of creation and their activities belong to Him and He influences them via each other.

Nevertheless, nothing in the micro or macro planes of existence can be labeled 'Allah'! Yet His existence in that unit can't be denied either! This is why the Rasul (saw) said, "You can't thank Allah if you don't thank the person!"

The giver is always Allah, as the verse evidences:

"Indeed, Allah is with those who have certainty (those who turn to Allah as though they see Him, i.e. the manifestations of the qualities of His Names)."[55]

This is the mystery of the unity of existence!

So, if you encounter one that gives and don't thank him, you'll only be thanking a god in your imagination instead…

Only after discerning this reality can one truly READ and understand the meanings denoted by the verses above…

The constellations of stars, i.e. the star signs, affect us and our world constantly via their cosmic rays…

The cosmic rays comprising some of the meanings of Allah's names that are radiated by the stars affect the DNA and RNA strands of all living beings, activating some of their genetic codes and instigating them in particular ways.

Ibn Arabi, one of the greatest of saints and masters of unveiling, says in his *Bezels of Wisdom*, "Everything that transpires and is to transpire in the world, the intermediary realm (*barzakh*) and the heavens, is formed via the effects of the star signs…" Thus, it is said divine determining comes from the sky.[56]

---

[55] Quran 29:69
[56] More on the life forms on other planets can be found in *Universal Mysteries*.

Life forms called 'angels' in religious terminology, who are unperceivable by us due to the different dimension in which they reside, affect us also. These have nothing to do with the jinn, who also live among us. But there's a great deception here...

The jinn, who, by the way, project themselves as aliens from outer space, also impose themselves as angels from time to time on those with whom they are in relation... Whether they claim to be aliens or angels, or claim to be Rumi or the spirit of someone else, they let us know with certainty that they are the jinn.

And the only definite way to be protected from them is with the following verses of the Quran:

"Rabbi annee massani ash-shaytaanu binuṣubin wa `adhaabin rabbi a`oodhu bika min hamazaati ash-shayṭaani wa a`oodhu bika rabbi an yaḥdurooni wa ḥifẓan min kulli shayṭaanin maaridin"[57]

Indeed, Satan (the feeling of being this body) **has given me hardship and torment.**

My Rabb (the protective Names within my essence)**, I seek refuge in You from the incitements of the satans** (that call to corporeality)**.**

And protected it (Earth's atmosphere) **from every rebellious Satan** (the purified consciousness is beyond the reach of illusory impulses)**.**

Detailed information and additional prayers for protection can be found in *The Power of Prayer*. If those who are afflicted recite these verses 150-200 times a day and the prayer provided at the beginning of *The Power of Prayer* 100 times a day, they can be sure to be safe from such effects.

---

[57] Quran 38:41, 23:97-98 and 37:7

Of course, this is provided they persist in reading these verses despite whatever distress and resistance befalls them while reading.

Allah's absolute will is in effect in the universe at every instance in the guise of astrological effects, to which we are subject at all times.

This transmission is what the word 'guidance' refers to, as it plays out in a most graceful way without us even noticing, manifesting the name Latif.

As the verse above – **"And He leads to the reality by the stars…"**[58] – evidences, guidance occurs through the channel of the stars. If we decipher the meaning of this verse in light of the letter B we encounter a very unique meaning:

"Allah the Guide (al-Hadi) makes His guidance reach them with the meanings of His Names via the effects-angels-rays that radiate from the objects He created called stars."

Though seemingly the effect is from the stars, in essence it is from Allah.

Just as we say "I ate, Allah gave me strength" or "I took medication, Allah gave me healing" etc.

Having covered the mechanism of guidance, let us now talk about the different types of guidance…

Note, however, talking about the measure of Allah's guidance denotes a limitation, which isn't possible. So then, to put it most comprehensively, the meaning of guidance entails the ease provided to the whole of creation so it fulfills its creational purpose. On the other hand, a more limited understanding can be defined as the ability to see the difference between actual truth and relative truth.

---

[58] Quran 16:16

As for the word SIRAT...

Generally, sirat is translated as path or road, thus the phrase 'sirat al-mustaqeem' can be understood as being on the path of Allah...

'Mustaqeem' denotes being straight, such that there is no left or right curvature, no ups or downs, like a laser beam that goes straight between two points.

Essentially, all of creation is on the path of Allah by default.

Indeed, "There are as many paths to Allah as the number of beings" and "everyone is under the administration of their own Rabb"...

Say, "Everyone acts according to his own creation program (natural disposition; fitrah)."[59]

Therefore, "Guide us to the straight path", based on the spirit of the Fatiha, is to say "Ease for us the way to fulfill our creational purpose."

There is a path that is suitable for everyone's purpose of creation...

The following verses elucidate that we ask for 'guidance' towards a 'blessed' path, one of eternal bliss and happiness, i.e. that we ask a lifestyle, based on the truths taught by Muhammad (saw), is eased for us...

"The path of those upon whom You have bestowed favor (those who believe in the Names of Allah as comprising their essential self and experience the awareness of their force) **not of those who have evoked Your wrath** (who have failed to the see the reality of their selves and the corporeal worlds and who have become conditioned with their ego-identities) **nor of those who are**

---

[59] Quran 17:84

astray (from the reality and understanding of the One denoted by the name Allah, the al-Wahid-ul Ahad-as-Samad, and who thus associate partners with Allah [shirq; duality])."

Essentially, such a blessed path formed by the grace of the Rahman is one that leads the person to his Rabb, his essential reality, and thus nothing can be a greater bliss than this!

Aside from this general blessing of Allah, there is also a more exclusive blessing...

According to the Quran, this blessing is granted to the righteous, the martyrs, the saints and the Nabis... They, degree by degree, attain closeness to Allah with this blessing, so 'guidance' can also be understood as that which leads to the path enabling divine closeness...

And who are **'those who have evoked His wrath'** and **'those who have gone astray'?**

Wrath can be conceived as the consequences of doing wrong, whereby the biggest wrong is one that is done to the self, which results in 'duality'!

Duality includes all ideas, thoughts and beliefs that denote a god besides Allah, the eternal and limitless Oneness!

All such concepts consequently spawn wrath... Therefore, this phrase refers to the people of duality, those who believe in the concept of an external deity-god.

Going astray, on the other hand, refers to diversion from the straight path either deliberately or inadvertently. That is, while being on the straight path, it is the act of either making a mistake or consciously diverting from the straight path to another direction.

If one has found the truth and is living upon the truth, then turns towards an idea or belief that leads them away from the truth, this is called 'going astray'…

Only Allah knows the absolute reality, of course, but according to my understanding **'those who have evoked His wrath'** refers to the people of duality, who believe in the concept of a deity-god, and **'those who have gone astray'** refers to the People of the Book, who have been notified of the truth but have then gone astray from the path of Allah, Islam, the only religion in the sight of Allah, or the teachings of Moses and Jesus.

This being the case, how to protect ourselves?

30

PROTECTION

As you probably noticed, the verse READ and those that follow it were all about what is and how to decipher the system.

Fatiha, on the other hand, is all about making man become conscious about the concept of Allah, the system of the universe and the mechanism to which mankind is subject.

Now, continuing on this, the first verses of chapter al-Baqarah talk about what one can do to protect oneself...

So then, what can we do? Which actions will result in which consequence within this system?

Let us try to answer this with the first five verses of chapter al-Baqarah:

1. Alif Lam Meem.

2. This is the Knowledge (Book) **of the reality and sunnatullah** (the mechanics of the system of Allah)**, about which there is absolutely no doubt; it is the source of comprehension for those who seek protection.**

3. Who believe in the reality (that their being comprises the compositions of the Names of Allah) **unknown to them** (beyond their perception)**, and who establish prayer** (who experience the meaning of salat alongside performing its physical actions) **and who spend unrequitedly from both the physical and spiritual**

sustenance of life that We have provided for them for the sake of Allah.

4. And who believe in what has been revealed to you from your essence (from the depths of your essence to your consciousness) **and what was revealed before you, and who, of their eternal life to come, are certain** (in complete submission as a result of an absolute comprehension).

5. They are in a state of HUDA (comprehension of the reality) **from their Rabb** (the Name composition comprising their essence) **and it is they who are successful.**

These verses, which outline the criteria to be successful, must be understood well, for, in order to apply something, one must first know what that thing is.

As can be seen, first and foremost it talks about the qualities and activities of those who 'seek protection'.

So, what needs to be done to reach success and salvation?

Let's begin with the first verse: "Alif Lam Meem."

These are symbolic expressions. Such symbols are used to denote realities that are beyond general human comprehension. Generally, the human mind can't evaluate things from multiple perspectives, like the blind men who, in the well-known story, try defining an elephant. As the story goes, each man feels one part of the elephant, then, when they compare their experience, they fall into dispute with one another. The one who touches the leg claims it's a pole, the one who touches its breast says it's a wall, the one who feels its trunk claims it's a snake, and so on...

Indeed, if the Quran is approached only from a single aspect and the universal system it discloses is evaluated only through a single perspective, such as the interpretations of the past, the metaphoric expressions of Sufism or only through the lens of science, the resulting situation will be no different to that of the blind men in the story!

Allah employs the language of symbols to prevent literal and shallow interpretations devoid of a holistic approach and to reward those who engage in serious contemplation – not to mention elucidating certain truths that were near impossible to be discerned in the past…

Let us know with certainty that it is not possible to understand the BOOK of universality and to decipher the secrets contained therein based on one field of expertise, unless one is bestowed divine aid and guidance!

On the contrary, an attempt to synthesize the multiple layers of meanings contained in the Quran in light of one field of study is sure to be misleading.

Neither scholars of Islamic jurisprudence nor interpreters, hadith experts, Sufi masters, doctors, physicists or mathematicians can infer the complete meaning of the Quran based only on their own field of expertise. This will only lead to serious deviation.

Thus, the safest and easiest approach is to acquire as much knowledge from as many fields as possible to enable us to understand the 'system' in the most comprehensive way. For this, we must first realize that nothing in nature is illogical or meaningless.

Now back to the symbolic letters: Alif Lam Meem…

Various ideas have been put forth by scholars in regards to the possible meanings of these letters… It is already known that these letters and others, such as "Qaf, ha, ya, ayn, sad" and "Ha, meem, ayn, seen, qaf", are letters among the Names of Allah and the Rasul (saw) used to pray with these Names.

Based on this, some have claimed these letters are also Names of Allah. On the other hand, Hadhrat Abu Bakr (ra) says, "Every book contains a secret of Allah. His secret in the Quran is contained in the preceding" and Hadhrat Ali (ra) says, "Every book has an essence, the essence of this book is in the syllables."

Ibn Abbas (ra) says, "Alif denotes Names and attributes such as 'Ahad, Awwal, Pre-eternal, Post-eternal', Lam points to His Latif attribute, Meem is a reference to his names and attributes 'Maleek, Maalik, Majid, Mannan'!"

Other interpretations are as follows:

"Alif points to Allah, Lam to Gabriel and Meem to Muhammad (saw)", i.e. that it means, "The word of Allah, the Quran, was revealed via Gabriel to Muhammad (saw)"...

"Alif symbolizes the 'I', Lam symbolizes Allah and Meem points to the name Aleem" to mean "I am Allah, the All-Knowing One".

My personal observation is that Alif points to the meaning of Ahad (Absolute Oneness), Lam designates *Uluhiyyah* from respect of the Latif and Meem points to the reality of Muhammad. Notice that 'Alif Lam Meem' is the first verse immediately after Fatiha, acting as a bridge between the two chapters.

Fatiha talks about the worlds and their places in the sight of Allah, the administration of Allah upon them and the fulfillment of their servitude with the aid of general and exclusive guidance.

These letters then summarize the fact that the Absolute One (Ahad) manifests His *Uluhiyyah* as the Latif, through the reality of Muhammad.

The first creation is the Grand Spirit. Some refer to the Grand Spirit as the First Intellect. The essence and origin of the spirit of the Rasul of Allah (saw) is this. At this point there are no individual forms and spirits.

In other words, these letters signify the manifestation of the One as the many through the reality of Muhammad, after which the detailed explanation of the many is provided throughout the chapter.

Ahad means infinite limitless Oneness besides which nothing else exists.

The absolute perfection comprised of Allah's infinite qualities comprises what is referred to as the *Uluhiyyah* of Allah, the Ahad. And this infinite perfection becomes manifest as the universe, that is, the reality of Muhammad!

Then, as an attribution to Meem, it says:

This is the Book (Knowledge) **of the reality and sunnatullah** (the mechanics of the system of Allah)**, about which there is absolutely no doubt; it is the source of comprehension for those who seek protection.**

Albeit 'the Book' is commonly understood as the Quran, I am of the opinion that it needs to be evaluated from the broadest perspective, in which case we can recapitulate the above verses as:

The magnificent system (Book) that encompasses such a perfect mechanism (based on the meanings of the Names of Allah and thus infinite wisdom and supremacy) that there is absolutely no room for any doubt (that there is a creator of Absolute Knowledge and Power).

Therefore, this book of the universe, in terms of its existence, makeup and mechanics, is guidance for those who contemplate, who READ the system and want to protect themselves.

Or, 'the Book' – i.e. the Quran – which reveals the system, is a source of guidance for those who seek protection, who are unable to read the system, yet who choose to believe and submit instead.

31

TAQWA

The word *taqwa* means to seek protection from a possible danger or anything that is likely to lead the person to suffering.

There are three levels of protection:

1. Protection from duality (*shirq*) – to take as deity things besides Allah.
2. Protection from mistakes or what is commonly referred to as 'sin'.
3. Protection from thoughts that are unbecoming of a servant of Allah.

As the first two are self-explanatory, I want to talk a little about the third level.

What is befitting a servant of Allah is to be conscious at every instance that he is comprised of the Names and attributes of Allah and the sole purpose of his existence is to be a servant of Allah, that he is 'nothing' in the sight of Allah (that his individual existence is an illusion) and thus to conduct his emotions, thoughts and actions independent of his ego... To be in constant observation of the fact that others are also manifestations of Allah's Names and attributes, and that Allah is the ultimate creator of all actions... Hence, to be in a state of protection at all times.

If we look at it from the broadest perspective, why do we need protection? And why has guidance been given not to the whole of humanity, but particularly to those who protect themselves?

Let's remember the verse:

"This is the Knowledge (Book) **of the reality and sunnatullah** (the mechanics of the system of Allah), **about which there is absolutely no doubt; it is the source of comprehension for those who seek protection."**[60]

Everything in the universal system of Allah is subject to the process of coming to life, reproducing and dying, in other words, transforming!

This being the case, it is imperative for one to consider what is awaiting after the transformation of death. Let's remember the exemplary reply Hadhrat Ali (ra) gave to one who asked him, "You ask me to prepare for the afterlife, O Ali, but what if none of what you claim actually exists? What if none of it is true?"

"If none of it is true then I have nothing to lose, but if the things the Rasul taught us are true and you've done nothing to prepare for them, can you imagine the state you'll be in forever? Can you fathom the loss you'll be in and are you conscious of the fact that you can never compensate for your losses?"

Put simply:

If you fear death, you don't jump off a tall building or go swimming in shark-infested waters, i.e. if your goal is self-preservation!

That is, seeking protection from danger is a natural instinct.

I find it quite striking that some claim they'll 'see about it' if life after death really does exist, that 'surely they'll find a way to manage'! If a man doesn't know how to swim, then wakes up and finds himself in the ocean, what's there to 'see about'? This is as absurd as saying, "I'll learn how to swim once I fall into the ocean!"

The Universal Book or 'System of Life' can only be discerned by READing and living by it. Many dangers await us in the life after

---

[60] Quran 2:2

death, against which any intelligent person would want to seek protection.

So, how to seek protection? What to do to be safe from these dangers?

32

WHAT IS THE UNKNOWN/UNSEEN?

"Who believe in the reality (that their being comprises the compositions of the Names of Allah) **unknown to them** (beyond their perception)**, and who establish prayer** (who experience the meaning of salat alongside performing its physical actions) **and who spend unrequitedly from both the physical and spiritual sustenance of life that We have provided for them for the sake of Allah. And who believe in what has been revealed to you from your essence** (from the depths of your essence to your consciousness) **and what was revealed before you, and who, of their eternal life to come, are certain** (in complete submission as a result of an absolute comprehension)**."**[61]

As can be seen from the above verse, one of the first criterions for protection is to have faith in the unknown.

The unknown refers to everything that falls outside our capacity of perception. When the brain is inadequate to perceive things outside the range of the five senses it classifies them as the unknown, while the things it can perceive is referred to as those in the 'Realm of Witnessing' (*shahadah*), which is evidently our current perceived world of matter.

The realm of matter is an assumed world conditioned by the data received through the five senses for, in essence, the universe is

---

[61] Quran 2:3-4

comprised of quants from which different layers of existence become manifest.

Every being in every layer of existence perceives its own dimension as matter. In other words, matter is not an absolute plane of existence, but a relative one, based on the perception of beings in all layers of life.

In this sense, even those who have passed on to the life after death are living in a relatively material world... As such, heaven and hell or the realm of the jinn are also 'matter' according to their perception.

In short, man is composed of two parts, his body and his consciousness. Consciousness can never be 'bodiless', whether it be a biological body or a holographic spirit body.

Man will indefinitely continue his existence as a unit of body + consciousness.

Because this knowledge was not known in the past, there have been many disputes in regard to whether one will have a body during Doomsday and the life after, and whether this body will be material or spiritual, etc... Continuing to engage in such outdated notions and arguments is no different to discussing the benefits of travelling by ox-cart in the presence of a helicopter or talking about the benefits of an hourglass while quartz technology is in use.

Such notions will have no significance for one who discerns the fact that 'matter' and everything beyond it are relative layers of a single holistic existence!

Based on our current sense of perception, this world is matter. When we die and move on to a radial body, that plane of existence is also going to feel like matter, based on the perception of that body.

Thus, we are forever going to live in realms that will seem to be matter, though their qualities may be different to one another, whatever these relative material planes may be called!

Now, the unknown is generally classified as two types:

1. Relative unknown

2. Absolute unknown

Everything I've been talking about above is of the first type.

Absolute unknown refers to the knowledge of Allah, as no creation can ever know and encompass the knowledge of Allah.

In terms of Absolute Essence, Allah is the absolute unknown. It is absolutely impossible to completely know, comprehend and contemplate the essence of Allah. No creation can perceive His Absolute Essence; they can only talk about His qualities based on His manifestations.

The unknown denoted in, "None but Allah knows the unknown" is the absolute unknown.

Relative unknown, on the other hand, can be known if Allah wills it so and this may be in various ways. Saints and enlightened ones who acquire states of unveiling and self-discovery and perceive things that are outside the normal range of perception do so based on this.

The most significant side to the relative unknown is that which pertains to the life after death. The realm of the grave, the intermediary realm (barzakh), the place of gathering (mahshar) the Bridge of Sirat, heaven and hell, all of these are examined under relative unknown.

As I've explained in detail in *Muhammad's Allah*, the realm of the grave is the plane of life that is experienced after the person leaves their biological body.

The intermediary realm is the plane of existence in which the Nabis, martyrs and some saints are currently living and sometimes gather and interact with one another.

The place of gathering (mahshar) is where everyone, including those who are either experiencing a hell-like or heaven-like state in their grave, and those who are freely roaming in the intermediary realm will gather and see the results of their worldly deeds.

The Bridge of Sirat is when the people escape to places referred to as heavens while the Earth is being engulfed by hell.

Depending on the power they've acquired via the recommended practices on the Earth, people will either temporarily experience hell or be confined to it indefinitely due to a lack of sufficient power.

Or, they will pass all of these stages and reach the plane of existence referred to as heaven with their vicegerency qualities where they can manifest whatever they may desire.

All of this, whose transpiration will perhaps take millions of years, has been referred to as the unknown.

However, the unknown according to mankind is different than it is according to the jinn and different for the angels... That is, unknown is not something specific to man, but applies to all forms of creation. Thus, it has been called 'relative unknown'.

Also, if we look at it in light of the letter B, the word unknown begins with the letter B in Arabic (*B'ilghayb*), in which case the above verse can be construed as:

"Who, as directed by the Names of Allah comprising their essence in their unknown, believe that their unknown is an absolute unknown that can never be comprehended and encompassed."

As for the word believe in "who believe in the unknown", it can be understood in two ways:

Belief based on authenticity: That is, the person has done the necessary research and authenticated his belief.

Belief based on intuition: Common to most believers, it is when the person believes based on his intuition, whether he accounts for it with this or that reason, essentially it is a pure belief formed by an intuitive feeling.

Aside from these two, there are also those who believe just because everybody else believes, which is an imitative belief.

And then, superior to all of these is the type of faith called 'ikan' (certainty), which we'll cover later.

In short, 'who believe in the unknown' denotes three types of belief, either based on conditioning, intuition or authenticity.

33

SALAT

"…and who establish prayer…"[62]

The word 'salat' can mean both supplication and the five daily prayers, and should be examined in both ways. That is, salat has personal and communal roles. The application of the five daily prayers can also be in a number ways. It can be performed, established, centralized or experienced continually.

Whether we take it as supplication or the five daily prayers, in both cases the activity transpires as thoughts in the brain. As I explained in *The Power of Prayer*, supplication or verbal prayer is directed brainwaves. Since it is not mandatory to know the meanings of the recited verses, daily salat is also an activity of the brain.[63]

This being the case, even the simplest performance of salat triggers and activates the Names and qualities of Allah comprising the brain via the recited verses, and hence directs and transmits waves to its surroundings, while also uploading them to the spirit.

When this individual practice is done in a congregation, its effects are much greater, for, when all the brainwaves of the congregation are directed towards a specific target, the resulting force is obviously more profound than when it's only through a single brain. Thus, we can say to establish salat means to channel powerful brainwaves to

---

[62] Quran 2:3

[63] More information can be found in the *Mystery of Man*.

145

produce beneficial outcomes for society... Congregational prayers done for rain or the millions of people praying during pilgrimage are such examples.

Daily prayers that are done in a congregation are also more powerful than individual ones, as can be seen in the words of the Rasul of Allah (saw):

"Salat done with a congregation is twenty-five times more profitable than one that is done alone."

As for the individual application of salat...

The 'performing' of salat is what we generally do every day. We stand for prayer, recite the necessary verses – most of us without knowing what they mean – perform the necessary actions and complete our worship. During this many different thoughts may cross our minds and we may inadvertently engage in them... This kind of salat is the act of simply complying by Allah's command; transforming faith from a sense into an action...

Nevertheless, even if one doesn't know the meanings, the energy (nur) of the recited verses is converted into radial energy and uploaded to the person's spirit, increasing his nur. Thus, to claim, "I don't know what I'm reciting so I might as well not pray at all" and to abandon salat based on this will be the person's greatest loss.

Sadly today, the establishment of salat has been reduced only to performing salat, not establishing it.

Whereas, the establishment of salat leads to ascension (miraj)!

The Rasul of Allah (saw) says:

"Salat is the believer's ascension!"

That salat is the ascension of a believer means salat is union with Allah!

It is to observe the nothingness of your assumed identity and realize Allah is the Ever-Living One.

If you can't duly apply salat, it means you cannot yet establish salat, for the lowest degree of establishing salat is '*ihsan*' (divine favor).

The Rasul of Allah (saw) explains ihsan as:

"Ihsan is to do your salat conscious of the fact that Allah can see you even though you can't see Allah!"

In simple terms, this has been described as entering the presence of Allah.

But we are always in Allah's presence! To not realize this and to think we're in His presence only during salat is nothing but a serious deviation that will eventually lead one to disbelief! The assumption that you're not in His presence when you're not doing salat implies He isn't present in that place; that He can't see you because He's somewhere beyond! Absolute nonsense!

This absurd view leads to the assumption of a god far in space or to deny His existence altogether.

Thus, it's imperative that we understand this well, for the Rasul (saw) says "Salat is the pole of religion." What kind of salat is he referring to?

A salat that is established is one that is done in a state of awe and reverence, which does not denote fear by the way, as fear is felt when one feels in danger as opposed to awe, which is felt in the presence of grandeur and magnificence. It is when one feels his nothingness in the sight of an extraordinary greatness and sublimity. Contemplating the word 'Allahuakbar' is sufficient for one to feel awe during salat!

For salat to be complete, there are few criteria that need to be met: **Purification from filth and dirt, physical purification (ablution), covering of private parts, time of prayer, intention and turning to the qiblah.**

Additionally, there are six conditions that must be applied during salat: Opening takbir, standing position (qiyam), reciting of Quran (qiraah), bowing (ruku), prostration and the final sitting position.

Purification from filth and dirt can be described as two types, one that is visible and one that is invisible. The latter is more significant for this is the type of filth the Quran refers to as the filth of duality.

For one to thoroughly turn to salat, he must be cleansed from the concept of duality, which is also of two types: one that is apparent and one that is hidden.[64]

On the contrary, it is debatable how beneficial it can be to turn to an assumed god in space without understanding the reality of the One whose name is Allah.

The second condition is to take ablution. Physically, this is done with water or with soil… Since ablution can be taken even with one glass of water or, in case of no water, by rubbing soil onto one's face and other parts of the body, clearly this isn't about physical cleansing.[65]

The spiritual component of ablution is to cleanse one's self from the deeds that have come about from one's senses and organs – or in other words, from accrediting deeds to yourself and thinking you created them. It is to come to the understanding that the One creates everything based on divine wisdom.

In fact, it is to not even condition the One by 'wisdom'!

Covering of private parts during prayer is different for men and women. At the level of the mind, covering means to cover one's personal and identity based conditionings, value judgments and emotions and to be objective and open to the knowledge of Allah. In other words, to cover one's ego! The ego is one's point of shame, which if it can't be thrown out altogether, it should at least be covered.

The right timing is a necessary factor for salat to be fulfilled, for you can only pray the salat of the time that you are currently in. All

---

[64] More information on duality can be found in *The Great Awakening*.
[65] More in the reality of ablution can be found in *The Mystery of Man*.

other salats you make other than the salat of that particular time are also beneficial practices. Externally, there are five known time periods for salat. Spiritually, the right time comes when one is cleansed from the ego and is ready to go into the divine presence selflessly!

Intention is part of preparation for salat; it is to consciously turn towards and make a decision. The purpose is to realize one's nothingness in the sight of Allah and to become His conduit, such that it is He who recites through the person.

Turning to the Kaaba. A deeper meaning is turning to Allah, for it is He who exists in all essences. It is to feel the real existence in the non-existence of one's ego. It is to recognize one's nothingness in the sight of Allah, the Absolute Unknown... This is how salat begins...

As for the criteria that must be met for salat to be fulfilled:

The opening *takbir* is to say 'Allahu Akbar' in order to commence salat. If the person can really say Allahu Akbar – contemplating the Earth, the galaxy and the infinite vastness of space and understand his place within this magnificent infiniteness, and discern that the Sublime Creator of this infinite greatness is beyond comprehension – salat will have commenced.

The proper application of this creates such awe that many may shiver and feel some form of rapture at this point, experiencing the annihilation of their ego and reciting the Basmalah and Fatiha, at which point the reciter will no longer be the person. It will be Allah doing hamd to Himself through the person! As the verse evidences, "It was not you who threw when you threw"!

This is the type of salat referred to as ascension; it enables the person to reach the essence of salat and allows him to observe the Qayyum within his being.

Bowing is to bend and lower one's self before the Reciter, for everything in existence is fulfilling its servitude under the command of the Reciter by actualizing their creational purpose.

Then it is said, "Samiallahu liman hamidah" i.e. "Allah has perceived the hamd of the one who is doing hamd!"

How can He not? It was He who was doing the hamd in the first place, though the tongue belonged to the servant!

Then going back to upright position we say, "lakal hamd kama yanbagheey li jalali wajhika wa li azimi sultaniq..." i.e. "Hamd belongs to You! I am impotent from duly evaluating the sublimity of Your countenance and the might of Your sovereignty!"

Then taking the Rasul (saw) as example and feeling total impotence, we delve into nothingness by going down to prostration! Prostration is where the nothingness of the entire existence in the sight of Allah is observed and felt.

Then we sit up and say, "Have mercy on us, forgive us, bestow Your mercy and grace"... Then we prostrate again, this time, the one who observed the inexistence of everything in the sight of Allah has now become inexistent himself, he has reached the state of nothingness. Then the sitting position is taken again, and the calling comes, "At tahiyyatu lillahi was salawatu wattayyibat!" The answer is directly from the Rabb to the Reality of Muhammad in his essence: "As salamu alayka ya ayyuhan nabiyyu wa rahmatillahi wa barakatuhu!"

Salam is rippled out from the Reality of Muhamamd in the person's essence to all the righteous ones who fulfill their servitude; those who have rid themselves of their egos!

"May salam be upon us and all the righteous ones who fulfill their servitude!"

And thus the ascension of the person takes place.

If the effect of this experience is carried to all times, then the person is said to be in a state of constant salat and constant observation... May Allah guide us to this state.

However, regardless of the depth and level of salat, one must never abandon the physical application of it. Just as we don't stop eating for this reason or other, we must also not stop praying for any reason. The physical application of salat is different, the spiritual aspect of it different, each has its own set of benefits. Just as we have different conditions that affect our body and consciousness, we're going to have a body and consciousness in all states of the life after, and so neglecting the needs of either one will result in consequences both here and in the life after death.

One who isn't a gnostic, one who can't read in the light of the letter B is generally veiled from the external with the light of unveiling. That is, the secrets that are unveiled to them blind them from seeing the external realities. Thus, they need to take the intimates of the reality in the past as examples and follow in their footsteps if they don't want to deviate from the truth and reach the path of gnosis. Otherwise, they can get locked into one observation and become deprived of the infinite gnosis that lies beyond it.

I hope I've been able to explain the meaning of "and who establish prayer"...

Now for the rest...

34

THE REASONS FOR CHARITY

"And who spend unrequitedly from both the physical and spiritual sustenance of life that We have provided for them for the sake of Allah."

The word 'sustenance' has a very broad meaning, entailing all things that can be eaten, used, consumed and benefitted from, as well as one's children, partner, work, knowledge and spiritual states…

Charity (*infak*) on the other hand means to spend from yourself to give to another. There are two types of charity. The first is to spend from the sustenance that you've been given, whatever portion it may be… The second type is defined as '*albirra*', which the following verse references:

"Never will you experience the essence of reality (*albirra*) until you unrequitedly give away that which you love."[66]

As can be seen, the condition is that you give away 'that which you love', not just random things.

When this verse was revealed, the companions of the Rasul (saw) immediately gave away their favorite possessions… Surely this

---

[66] Quran 3:92

verse is addressing all Muslims of all times until Doomsday, not just of that time.

But why must we give away from that which we have been given?

The prominent reason for charity is to rid one's self from the concept of ownership by sharing one's possessions with others. We're all going to have to give up the things we own at some point anyway, we're all going to leave this world and everything in it behind. So, the smart thing to do is to live conscious of this truth and not get possessive over anything. That which attaches man to this world most are the things he thinks he owns. Jesus says, "The heart of man is with the things he owns, so then give up the things you own for the sake of Allah that your heart may be with the Kingdom of Heaven!"

The biggest cause of suffering at the point of death, or transformation, is the feeling of losing one's possessions and loved ones. Islam provides the formula to prevent this suffering by telling you to give up everything you own for the sake of Allah and to realize it is He who gives and He who takes, and there is always wisdom in both cases. Islam tells us to live with this consciousness and to realize everything is given as a trust and thus to neither get overjoyed with what you're given nor distressed by what is taken from you.

Essentially, sustenance is completely determined by Allah, none has the right to ask how and why. He gives to whom He will as much as He wills and takes from whom He will as He wills...

A smart person is one who knows the giver and taker is always Allah and thus does not feel a sense of ownership towards anything!

He may inspire you to give to me and inspire me to give to another, whoever the seeming giver and taker may be, the real cause and determiner is always Allah, all else is only a vehicle.

None can give what is not determined and none can withhold what is. Once we understand this truth, giving charity will become very easy. Whether you understand charity as alms-giving or donation or as giving a gift, the important thing is to share with others without expecting something in return.

The underlying reason for expecting a return is again due to the feeling of ownership and thus the ego. If you give something that you think belongs to you then surely you will expect a return, but when you know you're not the owner then you cannot expect a return. If you return something that was given to you as a trust, can you expect a return? Obviously not! Thus, the only way to prevent expectation is to realize you're merely the keeper and not the owner.

Therefore, those who want to protect themselves must give charity, for the only way to prevent the suffering of loss is to practice the art of giving now.

A more profound degree of this is denoted in the above verse regarding *albirra*.

The only way to reach *albirra*, or to experience the essence of reality, is to abandon one's self or ego. If one is not identified as a person, then surely one cannot feel a sense of ownership, everything will become His. Wherever and with whomever your beloved may be, you will know that in reality they are with you, for they are always with Him! The sense of being a separate unit of existence will be removed and Allah will be sufficient.

Due to this, to physically give up the things you love is by essence giving up your ego and sense of personhood. And this is the key that opens the door to true union.

To sum it up, if you want to prevent the pain of loss during death, you must give charity, at least as the amount defined by almsgiving (*zakah*) or as much as you can to provide service to your community.

"He who does not thank the people cannot thank Allah!"

Give up your self for the sake of Allah!

35

RELIGION OR RELIGIONS?

"And who believe in what has been revealed to you from your essence (from the depths of your essence to your consciousness) **and what was revealed before you, and who, of their eternal life to come, are certain** (in complete submission as a result of an absolute comprehension).**"**[67]

Let's also remember the two verses previously shared:

"Indeed, the religion (system and order) **in the sight of Allah is Islam"**[68]

"And whoever seeks a religion (system and order) **other than Islam** (the consciousness of being in a state of submission) **his search will be ineffective!"**[69]

Notice in the first verse there is no time condition; it does not address a specific period of time. That is, it denotes that at all times and as long as mankind exists, there is only one system in the sight of Allah, accepted as religion, and that is Islam. This is what religion

---

[67] Quran 2:4
[68] Quran 3:19
[69] Quran 3:85

is. Islam is the religion valid from the time of Nabi Adam until Doomsday.

One may ask, "What about Judaism and Christianity and so on? Are they not classified as religions in the sight of Allah?"

If we understand the meaning of Islam well, we'll see that Moses and Jesus, among countless others, have all tried to explain the same system, but because the universality of their teachings was not discerned it was reduced to a tribal belief system. Thus, the Jews claim only the Jews will go to heaven and the Christians claim only the Christians will go to heaven, whereas we as Muslims say everyone who accepts the teachings of all the Nabis and Rasuls and who tries to follow their paths will go to heaven, whatever nationality or culture they may be from...

Or, more realistically, anyone Allah wills will go to heaven!

We believe in everything Allah's Rasul and final Nabi taught us, we also believe in the original teachings of prior Nabis and Rasuls, including Jesus and Moses.

We know they also informed their people of Allah and the religion and the lifestyle most appropriate to their time, according to how it was revealed to them by Allah.

There are two types of revelations in religion:

The first is absolute and not subject to change at any time.

The second is based on the conditions of that particular area and time, teaching the best ways of protection according to that region or time period. These have been updated and changed by different Nabis as times have changed.

So Islam is the absolute religion in the sight of Allah and applies to all times in terms of the absolute truths it discloses, yet in respect to the practical recommendations it makes to people, it is open to new developments.

Therefore, as well as believing in all the Nabis who have all brought the same message, we also confirm the original information contained in the books they brought.

We know that believing in Allah, life after death, the angels and that all deeds are accountable, is common to all faith systems. None of these are subject to change by time. On the other hand, recommendations at the level of social life have obviously changed, but this does not in any way mean that a new religion has come.

36

HAVING CERTAINTY IN LIFE BEYOND DEATH

"And who, of their eternal life to come, are certain"[70]

What does it mean to be certain of all the stages of the eternal life to come? What is certainty?

The eternal life to come or 'life after death' begins immediately after the experience of death. The person makes a transition from the dimension of life he perceives with his senses to a life with a luminous brain-body and continues to live in this plane of existence. He then moves on to the life of the grave or the intermediary realm, in which he continues to live until Doomsday. After this, those in the life of the grave and those in the intermediary realm will begin to live in a body that will be formed according to the conditions of the Doomsday period. This plane of life, also known as the Place of Gathering (*mahshar*), will then continue through the Bridge of Sirat to either hell or heaven.

"And there is none among you who He will not pass through (experience) **hell!"**[71]

---

[70] Quran 2:4
[71] Quran 19:71

Those who can pass and escape this stage will then be equipped with a new angelic body and continue their lives in paradise.

Those who believe in the Rasul of Allah (saw) need not only believe in all of these stages pertaining to life after death, but also have *certainty*.

What is certainty?

There are three statements regarding the state of certainty:

1. I know with certainty that this is so.
2. I have no doubt about this and won't have any doubt in the future.
3. It can't be any other way.

One who can say all three is one with certainty.

I explain and write about the stages of life after death because I'm certain of the teachings of Muhammad (saw)! In respect of all the information that has reached us, my own observations and modern scientific data, life after death is a definite fact without doubt! Thus, having certainty is to know no other possibility exists!

Therefore, to be 'certain of all the stages of the eternal life to come' is to know without doubt and without any room for debate that this is the absolute truth. Such people will then do everything they can to protect themselves.

Such are the people who have full faith in the eternal life to come and thus establish their salat, spend in the way of Allah from the sustenance they've been given, who believe in what has been revealed to Muhammad (saw) and to those before him, and who are certain of the eternal life to come.

They do this with the guidance given to them by their Rabb.

The word Rabb denotes the sublime power to which we owe our existence, the power that has created us and everything that transpires through us. It is with this power that we are able to continue our lives and conduct all our actions.

Without 'guidance', the ease of divine facilitation, we could not be of the people of faith.

So, let us know with certainty that, if we're of the believers, if we can comply with the recommendations of the Rasul of Allah (saw), this is entirely due to the guidance from our Rabb.

He who is unable to see this truth is called neglectful (*ghafil*) and cocooned. He who denies this truth is called a disbeliever (*kafir*); one who covers the truth, one who is ignorant of the reality. Such people are the most needy in any society, for out of their inability to understand and evaluate the reality, they lead themselves straight into suffering.

On the other hand, those who believe in Muhammad (saw) despite not being able to read the system and those who can read the system and thus have attained certainty, they are the ones who will be able to overcome all obstacles and reach true success! They are those upon whom Allah has bestowed his favor.

37

AN ESSENTIAL EXPLANATION REGARDING THE SYSTEM

In his *The Holographic Universe*, Michael Talbot presents the theories of Bohm and Pribram, and in reference to their proposed new way of looking at the world, he says:

"Our brains mathematically construct objective reality by interpreting frequencies that are ultimately projections from another dimension, a deeper order of existence that is beyond both space and time: The brain is a hologram enfolded in a holographic universe."[72]

Let's try to understand the implications of this powerful view. First of all, let's put time and space aside, and focus on the words:

"... A deeper order of existence from another dimension." A **'deeper'** order is the order within the depths of our existence; our essence, in Sufi terms, the **Absolute Existence!**

Beyond the illusory existence that we refer to when we say **'I'**, exists another **'I'**, one that is common to all existence, the Absolute **'I', the Absolute Self!**

The brain, then, is the converter of the frequencies that are projections from this Absolute 'I', who projects the frequencies of His implicit meanings that He wants to disclose!

I cannot adequately stress the importance of the following:

---

[72] Talbot, 1991

"Allah has created each person for a particular purpose. Only by complying with their natural disposition (*fitrah*), and following the path that is best suited to their makeup, can people fulfil their unique purpose. It is this fulfilment that renders their servitude accomplished!"

If we can truly grasp the meaning of and internalize this truth, we can no longer feel angered, depressed, annoyed or critical! For we will be cognizant of the reality that each person can only disclose their own natural disposition, regardless of whether their disposition complies with or contradicts ours! It is as absurd to question another's motives, as it is to question the liver as to why it doesn't pump like the heart!

Indeed, this truth is the essence and the summary of the system and the order as described by the Quran.

As long as someone fails to comprehend this reality, their claims to believe in Allah are false; their faith is only an imitation.

Real faith is the fruit of the comprehension, internalization and application of this reality.

First of all, a Sufi aspirant **must abandon his anger!** For, as soon as one is angered by something, one is veritably dismissing and denying Allah! Each individual can only execute what is in his creation program. To become infuriated by another is no different than being infuriated by the disposition assigned to him by Allah, i.e. **the decree of Allah**.

If Allah has willed to create that individual with that particular program, how can we question His absolute knowledge and will? Clearly, Allah has deliberately chosen to designate that particular composition to that particular individual. To think they are wrong, or flawed or inappropriate, is to undermine, doubt and even deny the Godhead of Allah!

Question: *What do dreams signify? Do they have a valid place in the system? How do we see what we see in our dreams? Do our spirits leave our body and go elsewhere?*

The term **'astral travelling'** denotes a state of the brain, where the emission of a certain kind of radar waves projects certain images to our brain, allowing us to see and experience certain things or events.

The general concept is that the spirit leaves the body when we sleep, takes a little tour, then re-enters at the time of waking. This isn't so! The spirit does not leave the body or go anywhere! The enlightened ones, who have been able to activate their third eye, have mastered the ability to direct their radar waves to a particular location and perceive that place through images that get projected back to their brains.

Those who are ignorant of the mechanics of this process think their spirits actually leave their body and go to some other place.

Whereas the spirit can only leave the body in two ways:

1. Death

2. Self-conquest (*fath*)

The truly enlightened ones, who have been able to conquer their souls, who have **'died before death'** and attained the state of *haqq al-yakeen* (the certainty of the reality), are the only ones who can observe without the body. All other observers rely on the radar waves emitted by their brain![73]

The **radar waves** can either be miracle-based and directed to the material dimensions above **Earth**, or phenomenon-based and directed to the dimensions of **heaven, hell** and **the intermediary realm.** It can also be directed towards lower dimensions, depending on the expansion capacity of the brain.

To give an example, when we dream of angels, we see them in various forms and figures with which we are already familiar.

Angels do not have 'forms' in their original state; they only have certain frequencies in relation to their particular function. In other words, angels are 'high frequency vibrations'. **When one of these frequencies reaches our brain, we crosscheck it with our**

---

[73] This topic has been covered in detail in my book *The Power of Prayer* for those who may be interested.

pre-existing database and decode it based on the closest frequency we can find, and then assign an image to it.

When a tree talks in our dream, for example, it's actually an angel; a high frequency vibration that is decoded and interpreted as a tree, as this is the closest frequency the brain is able to find in its database!

As such, when various incoming frequencies reach the brain, an automatic search engine is activated to find the closest corresponding match to 'define' it. Whatever form has already been assigned to that closest match remains unchanged. Hence, we see dreams in symbols and not in their original state.

If we take it a step further... **Muhammad (saw)** says: **"People are asleep and will be awakened with death!"**

What does this mean? If this life is like sleep, then we must all be dreaming! **This world, and everything in it, is like a dream in respect of the afterlife...** Everything we experience here, the pain, the joy, our possessions, our loved ones... All of it is going to feel like a dream when we wake up to the afterlife with death... And just like we perceive dreams, in the form of symbols as a result of our brain's frequency converting mechanism, so too we perceive everything in this dimension by the very same process.

All of this is confirmed by the world's leading neurophysiologist, Stanford University professor Karl Pribram, and the world famous physicist, David Bohm.

Question: *Can people have different perceptions of the same object?*

If the same frequency reaches two different people with the same database, then the resulting evaluation will be the same. This is precisely why we all perceive and see the same objects in the same way, because we all have the **same perception mechanism** and have been conditioned to function in pretty much the same way!

The visible spectrum, that is the frequency range that can be detected by the human eye, is definite. Whether the same frequencies reach one eye or 1,000 different eyes, the result will always be the same. They will all see the same thing, as all of them will be processing the incoming data using the same system.

Question: *Why does color-blindness result in different perceptions of colors?*

This is because, in the case of color-blindness, there is also a **difference** in the **mechanism of the brain**. That is, a person who is color-blind processes the incoming frequencies differently than a person who isn't. It's not that they receive different frequencies; it's that they possess different brains! The database, i.e. the accumulation of data during one's lifetime, is what defines the brain's capacity.

When we are born, our database consists only of **genetic** and **astrological data**, but as of birth, we are constantly prone to new information, new conditionings, and new data. This is why a newborn baby has limited vision, not because of a lack of sight, but because of the **lack of data** in the brain to 'evaluate' the information.

We can only project outwardly what we possess inwardly. Our ability to decipher a certain input of data depends solely on the database we have been building since our birth.

For example, the tendency to be fond of and drawn to beauty is a property of the brain. It may be related to either genetic traits or astrological influences, such as the position of Venus in one's natal chart. In any case, how this inclination externalizes in Iran is different to how it is expressed in Africa or Japan or the United States of America. Depending on how **environmental conditionings** shape one's database, traits that are primarily common to the whole of humanity become externalized through innumerably various means.

Question: *Are 'heaven' and 'hell' states of particular frequencies?*

All information or 'data' in our database is particular **frequencies**. One's experience of heavenly pleasures is directly proportionate to how rich and comprehensive one's database is. Hence, the different levels of heaven!

This is why **Muhammad (saw)** encourages the aspiration of knowledge with his words:

"Seek knowledge from the cradle to the grave", for the acquisition of knowledge is what increases the capacity of our database that exists in our brain and gets uploaded to our spirit. Our experience of life is the result of the information contained in this database. The quality and abundance of knowledge that we supply to it is what defines our 'experience' of life, and whether it is hell-like or heaven-like.

The Sufis say: *"Abstain from conversing with the foolish!"* Who are the foolish? **Those who are ignorant of their ignorance!**

Why must one 'abstain'? Simply because such people cannot add anything to an aspirant of knowledge. An aspirant should befriend those whose knowledge is greater and further than his, approaching the contrary only with the intent to share his knowledge.

An aspirant seeks to accumulate knowledge with the same eagerness that a worldly person seeks to accumulate money and wealth, as he denies the afterlife. This is because an aspirant knows he cannot attain any more knowledge; hence, develop his spirit any more after the point of death. This is why it is crucial for the aspirant to take heed of his masters' words: **"Seek knowledge from the cradle to the grave"**, **"Seek knowledge even if it is in China"**, **"Befriend those who are ahead of you in knowledge!"**

Commodious knowledge is knowledge that is useful after death, whereas **useless knowledge serves no purpose in the afterlife**. When the enlightened ones warn us against the attainment of useless knowledge, they are not prohibiting the acquisition of such knowledge altogether but, in fact, advising us not to be fixated or obstructed by it. For all encountered knowledge serves some purpose in life and nothing is encountered by coincidence.

All things experienced by creation are inclusive of their preordained purpose and program. Nothing is without reason. We are all individually equipped with the necessary program to fulfill the purpose the Creator has willed for us. We cannot execute a code that isn't written in our kernel!

Let me give an example from myself...

When I was around the age of 15-18, I thought of myself as a highly intelligent person. I often wondered why Allah willed for me to be born in Istanbul and not in a more developed country, such as some place in Europe or the USA. I even thought it would have been more fitting if I were born in Mecca or Medina. What was the wisdom behind this will?

After many years, I realized, if I had been born and raised in Mecca or Medina, my religious apprehension would probably not have surpassed the 'literal', disabling me from deciphering the symbolic and metaphoric nature of religion. If I was born in the West, on the other hand, I would probably have become a great scientist, *deprived* however of the knowledge imparted by **Muhammad (saw)**.

Allah willed for me to be born in Istanbul instead, a city on the **border of the East and the West**, right in the middle of both worlds! Thus, I was able to benefit from the teachings of the East and the resources of the West, forming a synthesis of both. I would probably have been deprived of this had my place of birth on the map been a little more on the left or a little more on the right!

As such, Allah designates the perfect environment and resources required for the fulfillment of every individual's unique purpose.

All of the above is based on a view going **from the Essence to the outer**.

If we employ the counter view, and look at **the Essence from the outer reality**, we may reversely conclude that the people in our lives, our environment and our occupation are all a herald of either good news or a catastrophe.

When viewed this way, interesting things come to mind! One no longer feels the need to say **'I wish...'** for one realizes with conviction that everything is exactly the way it is meant to be and always will be! It is useless to say **'I wish I hadn't done such and**

such mistake in the past'. Indeed, that mistake had to be done, those lessons had to be taken, those emotions had to be lived and everything had to occur in the exact way it did for us to discover ourselves and accomplish our purposes.

Mistakes and sins teach us valuable lessons. By repenting, we can be cleansed from the sin, but the lessons we learn will forever be ours to keep. Life is a journey we must take to reach the destination of our purpose. **Everything that is encountered on this journey, including the mistakes we make, is there to aid and guide us in that direction.**

Imagine a staircase of a billion steps. If your purpose in life is to constitute the 22,222nd step, then that is exactly where your life experience is going to lead you. Through the people you meet and the events you live, Allah is going to shape you and sculpt you to befit that particular position, not one more or one less.

Allah, in His Pre-Eternal Knowledge, has designed such a magnificent staircase called 'humanity' where each person is preordained to constitute one particular step; no one can escape his role or position in this miraculous staircase.

Sooner or later, each person will play out his role and constitute the step that has been assigned for him. Once the staircase is completed, Doomsday will occur.

Although I mentioned the word 'preordained', let us also be aware of the verse:

"At every instance HU (the Absolute Essence of Existence) **manifests Himself in yet another way!"**[74]

That is to say, Allah is present in every dimension, through the various forms within that dimension.

As such, just as it is true there is no **'free will'** and **only Allah's will**, it is equally true that every individual lives with their own will.

Though they seem to be opposite extremes in contradiction with one another, in fact, they are two sides of the same reality. It's not that there is the greater will of Allah and the lesser will of the

---

[74] Quran 55:29

people. In its essence, there is no distinction between the two; the distinction arises only by perception. That is, when viewed through the five senses, there is dispersion, hence many wills. When viewed through consciousness, there is unity, hence only **One will**. Consequently, one may claim, "There is a greater will pertaining to Allah" and this will be true, but one may not claim, "There is also a lesser will pertaining to man" or vice versa, as they are different impressions of the *same* thing.

In the realm of consciousness, there are no parts or monads, there is only the whole. What appears to be multiplicity is only the different relations and expressions the Names of the One assume. Hence, when we say 'also' we are denoting 'another' in addition to the One, which is implicative of *duality* (shirq; associating another being with Allah).

Like the staircase we mentioned above, if we eliminate a single step from the staircase, would it mean anything on its own? *Together* the steps form the staircase; they have no substantial existence on their own, as a single step does not lead one anywhere. The will of the One is like the staircase; the individual steps that compose it are not *separate* or *different* from it. Thus, what we refer to when we say **'individual will'** is essentially no different than the ultimate One will. As this staircase continues to evolve and extend, different manifestations appear. The verse, about Allah disclosing Himself in different ways every day, is in reference to these manifestations.

When Allah's attribute of life is reflected on us, we say "I'm alive". Our immortality is in respect to our source of life, being the life attribute of Allah. The same can be said about our knowledge, will, power and so on.

If we can change the direction of our view and start looking at things from the core rather than the outer shell, we may actually realize that everything we manifest is from Allah and submission to this divine guidance will inevitably take us to the actualization of our potentials.

The pre-ordainment, which we have discussed, does not in any way suggest that we sit back and do nothing as everything is already predetermined! The system does not allow inactivity! One who is static cannot survive in the system, just as the primary cell, formed by the sperm and the egg, would not have amounted to anything if it had said, "I have already been preordained to be a human being, so there is no need for me to undergo division and proliferation..." Indeed, it is impossible for the cell not to proliferate. It goes against its nature; it can't help but multiply!

In just the same way, we can't help but be ourselves. Whichever step we have been ordained to be in the staircase of humanity, we will be!

The ultimate destination is contained in the primary cell of our being. That cell contains my characteristics, i.e. by genotype and phenotype, but it doesn't define me in every detail.

When we look at things from an astrological view, for example, we say that we are currently under the effect of Uranus, where Uranus reflects the traits of Aquarius. This does not mean we can conclude from this that "Hulusi is going to write a book" or "Hulusi is going to contemplate on such and such".

The incoming new **wave** from Uranus will definitely **stimulate certain thought processes, but the results will vary among individuals according to their already existing databases.** If my database is ready to output a new thought, then the incoming stimulus will have a favorable effect on my intellect. But if I lack this capacity or am not in a receiving mode, then the same wave will come to me but have no effect on my brain function. The various planetary influences that reach the brain are nothing more than stimuli to activate certain parts of the brain.

Another example can be given of medical experiments performed on cats. Sexual activity of cats was observed to increase significantly when the sex centers in their brains were stimulated with electrodes. When their anger centers were stimulated, they started to growl. Thus, it can be understood that when certain sections of the brain are 'irritated', the brain responds. Likewise, when astrological data reaches the brain it comes in an elementary format, without a particular notion. Depending on which part of the brain receives the data, how it processes it, the contents of its database, and the interpretation it makes, the resulting behaviors differ.

As for fate...

A final destination and general path to lead us there have been predetermined for us. Everything else depends on the individual program we run and its natural consequences. Our program is constantly in sync with the angelic influences coming from our dimensional depths. Hence, our behavior is a synthesis of both the inward and outward influences that constantly surround us.

This formation is what we call **'individual will'**. To deny individual will is to deny this formation! To say individual will and the 'will of the One' are 'one and the same thing' is not to deny individual will; just as claiming ice to be water doesn't negate the formation called 'ice' (but doesn't assign a *separate* existence to ice either).

When we observe the reality from the dimension of pure consciousness, we cannot see anything in existence other than the One. In this state, there is no dispersion or multitude; there is no 'other' to possess a separate will. Only when we observe from an individual point of view, that is the dimension of multiplicity, we see individualized expressions of the One will, which appear to be many, but, in essence, they come from the same source.

The Quran elucidates this matter to those of understanding by saying **"You will only live the consequences of your own actions"**, referring to the individual will in the domain of multiplicity. Then, reflecting it from the projection of unity, it says **"There is only one will: Allah"**, referring to the reality that **"there is no existence other than Allah"**.

Both are true, as both are different projections of the same reality.

Note that the verse says **"Every day He manifests Himself in yet another way"**; it does not say 'Allah'. He is translated from the Arabic word **'HU'**, which does not connote gender, of course, but a pure being beyond description.

We can think of *HU* as the dimension of unity in the essence of each monad, the source of the constant formation.

HU is the unity disguised as multiplicity. HU is the dimension of oneness implicit in the essence of all things!

Question: *Is the acquisition of knowledge in our control? How does it affect our future; the 'step' we have been destined to compose?*

Knowledge, experience and guidance shape us into becoming the 'step' we are meant to be. The degree to which someone acquires and applies knowledge is the degree of 'shaping' that occurs. Without getting shaped, one cannot become. Therefore, knowledge without application is futile.

Let's say, for example, that I have attained much knowledge and internalized the fact that each individual can only express their natural disposition and can't display behavior beyond the limits of their capacity. Now, let's suppose I go to a restaurant, the waiter comes and throws the menu at me. Can I get angry or yell at him? He is only displaying the behavior resulting from his internal program; obviously he lacks the data to enable him to act in a different way!

If I were ignorant of this truth, I would react with anger and frustration. I would question his behavior with fury and try to correct him. Knowledge enables me to remain calm, to not react with emotions. Knowledge saves me from the unnecessary burdens of impulsive reactions and the tiresome repercussions arising as a result.

When a person gets infuriated and angry, millions of cells are terminated instantly! One moment of anger, depending on its intensity, can cause millions of short circuits and explosions at the molecular level, sometimes even damaging irreplaceable brain cells! So, how can a learned person who has acquired knowledge display such behavior and cause his own demise? Could this be true knowledge? If knowledge does not prevent us from harming ourselves and others, if knowledge does not 'shape' us, then we cannot really claim to have knowledge.

The cut of a diamond is what determines its value. A one-carat diamond with 52 facets is much more valuable than the same diamond with 32 or 16 facets. **The more a diamond is cut, the more its value will increase.**

We, also, are like diamonds. The more knowledge cuts and shapes us, the more we increase in value.

Question: *If the level of knowledge that I can acquire is up to me, that is, if I'm in charge of using my brain to evaluate knowledge, then it's logical to assume the 'step' we form in the staircase is not fixed, which means the staircase itself is not stable?*

Our place in the staircase is fixed. The place we occupy, the 'step' we compose, is the very purpose of our creation. However, its final shape is determined at the point of death. So long as we are living, we are still being cut and shaped.

As for the 'shaping' that happens in hell, it is like a final cleansing of the residues of impurities we carry from our worldly life. Like purifying gold with fire, it doesn't add any further value to it; only purifies it.

As such, **hell is not a place of getting shaped, but rather, it is a place of purification**.

Hellfire purifies and solidifies the things we've gained in the world, so we may enter heaven as refined beings.

No matter what the apparent reason may be, everyone experiences an intermediate phase in their lives, during which they suffer an internal burning. This burning, referred to as 'hellfire', is a way of cleansing ourselves from inappropriate states that impede our heavenly existence.

Those who are destined to stay in hell forever will also eventually reach a state of refinement after intense and extended suffering.

But, at the end of all suffering, the fire will be extinguished, the burning will end, and **new life will spring from the ashes**.

38

EPILOGUE

In this book, I have tried to share some of my research and observations with you.

We explored the first five verses of the Quran, the first revealed chapter and the first verses of chapter *al-Baqarah*, regarding the principles of protection (*taqwa*).

The accuracy of my understanding and construal is up to the judgment of the qualified... However, I shall be contented even if I've only been able to express the importance of approaching things with a broad view, free from narrow-mindedness.

Though I'm also aware that some self-acclaimed alleged 'scholars' of late may criticize my point of view and my attempts to evaluate things in light of science, it does not matter... They also constitute a place in this beautiful garden of life!

On the other hand, my advice to those who claim they don't understand these topics is to continue practicing their salats, and to continue fasting, going to pilgrimage and giving charity (zakah). For, just as our lack of understanding of the molecular makeup of the food we consume does not prevent us from becoming nourished, not understanding the details of these practices will not prevent us from their benefits.

This is the age of advanced technology. Worldwide communication has reached profound levels and the propaganda against the truth has entered each household, whether we accept this or not. No one can get anywhere by forbidding and censoring. I believe all such restrictions are going to be overcome in the following years. So, if we want to serve future generations in the way of Muhammad (saw), we must interpret religious teachings in the light of science, in a way that addresses the intellect and logic. The path to serving Islam goes through the principle of "Do not make things difficult, make it easy, do not discourage, instead invite to love".

Modern man is unaffected by and will only laugh at absurd statements such as, "This is so and you must accept it to be so otherwise you're a disbeliever!"

If we sincerely want to serve in the way of Islam and help modern man and the new generation to understand these truths, we must address them from their own world, in their own language, and present things in a logical way without contradiction.

As an Islamic intellectual and a Sufi, I would be gratified to know I've been of benefit and apologize for any mistakes I may have made, may Allah guide us to the reality.

The absolute truth is that I confirm everything the servant and Rasul of Allah, Muhammad (saw) taught us and I dedicate myself to his service. May Allah be our *Muin*!

Ahmed Hulusi
17 September 1992
Antalya

ABOUT THE AUTHOR

Ahmed Hulusi (Born January 21, 1945, Istanbul, Turkey) contemporary Islamic philosopher. From 1965 to this day he has written close to 30 books. His books are written based on Sufi wisdom and explain Islam through scientific principles. His established belief that the knowledge of Allah can only be properly shared without any expectation of return has led him to offer all of his works which include books, articles, and videos free of charge via his web-site. In 1970 he started examining the art of spirit evocation and linked these subjects parallel references in the Quran (smokeless flames and flames instilling pores). He found that these references were in fact pointing to luminous energy which led him to write *Spirit, Man, Jinn* while working as a journalist for the Aksam newspaper in Turkey. Published in 1985, his work called '*Mysteries of Man (Insan ve Sirlari)*' was Hulusi's first foray into decoding the messages of the Quran filled with metaphors and examples through a scientific backdrop. In 1991 he published *The Power of Prayer (Dua and Zikir)*' where he explains how the repetition of certain prayers and words can lead to the realization of the divine attributes inherent within our essence through increased brain capacity. In 2009 he completed his final work, '*Decoding the Quran, A Unique Sufi Interpretation*' which encompasses the understanding of leading Sufi scholars such as Abdulkarim al Jili, Abdul-Qadir Gilani, Muhyiddin Ibn al-Arabi, Imam Rabbani, Ahmed ar-Rifai, Imam Ghazali, and Razi, and which approached the messages of the Quran through the secret Key of the letter 'B'.

www.ingramcontent.com/pod-product-compliance
Lightning Source LLC
Chambersburg PA
CBHW031956040426
42448CB00006B/379